MW00958272

SLAYING
THE MOUSE

*A true story of healing in
the spiritual realms*

Second Edition

Wendy S. Halley

© 2012, 2006 Wendy Stofan Halley

All rights reserved. No part of this book may be reproduced or transmitted in any form or by any means without permission by the author.

Slaying the Mouse: A true story of healing in the spiritual realms (Second Edition)
ISBN 978-1-300-09067-0

Cover and interior design: Ellen Kiyler
Cover art: Wendy Halley
Poem: Wendy Halley

For Tim, one of my favorite human beings

acknowledgments

I have a lot to be thankful for.

I give thanks to my husband, John, whose support is unwavering and for being the coolest person I've ever known. To my Dad, for his love and tolerance of my "unusual" nature. And I give thanks to my little brother Tim for being such a wonderful friend, and for his trust in me.

I would like to thank my teachers in this world and in the spirit world. In the physical realm, my gratitude to my teachers Hank Wesselman and Jill Kuykendall is immense. Hank and Jill have shown me nothing but enthusiastic encouragement. They gave me room to spread my ethereal wings and fly – as long as I promised to come back.

Thank you to Steve and Henny the laughing frog.

A special thank you to my old friend Ellen Kiyler for offering to help me design yet another book cover, and to Anne Dillon for her editing expertise, patience, and kindness.

Working with Jason was an invaluable experience on many levels. I'm deeply grateful to him and to his family for giving me the opportunity to stretch myself in new and powerful ways.

Thank you... thank you... thank you...

introduction

L ate one Sunday morning in the spring of 2003, I received an unexpected phone call from my father. As soon as I heard his voice, I knew something was wrong. He told me that he had just gotten off the phone with my brother Tim, who was on his way to the hospital. Dad explained that Tim's girlfriend's nineteen-year-old brother Jason* mysteriously slipped into a deep coma and that his prognosis was grim.

"The family is hoping you can help," Dad said. "Tim told them about the shaman stuff you do."

My thoughts quickly ping-ponged from *absolutely, I'll help*, to *man, I hope I can do this*. I felt a strong desire to be of service to Jason and his family, but feared that I might not be skilled enough to pull it off. At the point when I received my dad's phone call, I was five years into an intense shamanic apprenticeship. I'd worked with many people who were in need of healing, but the greater part of my experience involved working with wounds of the heart and mind. Though my experience working with folks struggling with life threatening physical conditions was limited, my desire to help far outweighed my apprehension.

* *To protect the family's privacy, identifying information has been changed.*

I imagine that every novice of this ancient practice wrestles with similar fears. For tens of thousands of years, indigenous healers the world over have been "journeying" with their consciousness to the spirit world, or what some aboriginal people call the dreamtime, in order to commune with helping spirits for the purpose of healing and divination. These gifted visionaries and healers, commonly referred to as shamans, serve as bridges to the spiritual realms for the benefit of the members of their communities.

My own journey down this path began in 1998, although I didn't know it at the time. After a series of unusual visionary experiences (a story for another book), I was hungry for knowledge that would help me make sense of it all. I later received the foundation of my shamanic training from authors Hank Wesselman and Jill Kuykendall, whose powerful work is founded in the ancient Kahuna wisdom of Hawaii.

The shamanic path is a challenging one – a spiritual bootcamp of sorts. I quickly learned that the more I surrendered, the more profound my visionary experiences became... and the more I changed in response. The learning was deep, all consuming, and sometimes quite messy. The biggest challenge, for example, included getting past my big fat Western mind – which, at first, incessantly rolled its eyes at the notion that I could actually have conversations with animal and plant spirits, dead folks, and a whole host of benevolent spiritual entities. Once I took that mental leap, I was able to yield to the ethers and to begin establishing relationships with my spirit helpers. Life hasn't been the same since.

The story you're about to read is the true account of my nine-month dreamtime relationship with Jason while he was in various stages of a coma. (Please keep in my mind that this story is based solely on my perception of what transpired.)

Most of the narrative takes place in the realms of the spirit world. Interspersed throughout the narrative are the actual e-mails I received from my brother Tim, his former girlfriend, and her family. These communications will give you glimpses of what was going on in physical "everyday" reality. When I first released *Slaying the Mouse* six years ago, the story was incomplete and left readers wondering what happened to Jason. With this new edition, the story now has an ending.

Slaying the Mouse is about possibilities. My hope is that this story will leave you wondering about the nature of reality and inspired by human potential.

Wendy Halley
Northfield, Vermont

when I was young
squirming and crawling
my towering world
perfect and tame
made my smile leafy green

i was unaware of the coming wind
the bottom of my feast
the end of slow winding travels
soon the others disappeared
and with them, the light

alone, paralyzed
stiff in a coffin of my own making
the beginning
disguised as the end
i panicked and pleaded
"please just one more chance
to see the sun, to taste the green"
but with my pleas came darkness
as thick as molasses

abandoning my dreams
i surrendered into black
the stillness
vibrating with movement
folding in on itself
until I'm nothing…
and everything
i can fly.

1

J ason watched his body from across the room. It lay there motionless on the hospital bed. A monitor beeped to the rhythm of his heart while a machine pumped air in and out of his lungs. He found the scene creepy and surreal, especially the sound of his breathing. There was nothing human about it.

He gave up trying to get his family's attention when they were in the room. He wanted to tell them that he was okay. But they couldn't hear him. At least they couldn't hear the version of him that was screaming to get their attention. They just stared at his body, eyes clouded with fear and tears. They gently shook his body and talked to it, looking for some sign that he was going to wake up.

Jason's confusion was monumental. Questions spun in his head like desert brush caught in a dust devil. *Am I dreaming? Hallucinating? Am I having an out of body experience? Am I dead?* No answers came, just panic.

He watched as medical staff poked and prodded his body. He heard them talk about him as if he wasn't there. They said things like "spinal meningitis" and "encephalitis." After mulling over various "itis'es" they spoke about "brain damage" and "a persistent vegetative state," as if they were talking about structural "damage" to a building or the declining "state" of the economy.

His thoughts raced around the room, ricocheting off walls and slamming back into him. *Was I in an accident? Am I sick? Shit, is this really happening?*

At times he paced. Jason didn't know exactly how he did this, since you need legs to pace, and his were still attached to the body – his body – which happened to be lying on a hospital bed on the other side of the room.

Sometimes he floated around the room. A familiar sensation. Maybe from childhood. Other times he sat in the chair at the foot of the bed and stared at himself.

His awareness seemed to drift in and out. The moment he thought he knew what was happening he'd be somewhere else. His new baseline was disorientation. He didn't know what day it was or how much time had passed since all this began. It seemed like time was all at once slipping by, and yet it was taking so long for it happen.

He knew that there was something very wrong, but he had difficulty understanding what it was. It was as if his concept of himself was covered with a heavy grey membrane that suffocated any attempt to ponder his situation. At times, he had a faint glimmer of who he used to be. But Jason was finding it hard to remember that until a week ago, he was a healthy college student making music, hanging out with his friends, and planning his future.

His perceptions shifted incessantly. It was when he looked at his body lying lifeless on the hospital bed that he remembered that he was a nineteen-year-old guy named Jason. But when his awareness drifted away from physical reality, which happened more and more as time went on, his consciousness melted into a vast display of shapes and colors.

A strange routine developed as Jason tried to keep his focus on the physical. He started recognizing nurses and doctors as they came and went, on and off their shifts. He found that he felt more stable if he focused on them. After a while he began to see into them, to see their intentions. He could discern each person's truth – from the people who truly wanted to help to those who were easily annoyed and eager to get off work. Their intentions appeared like clouds of light billowing from their bodies. He noticed that the people who wanted to help were bright like stars with far-reaching rays. And the miserable fucks, who were putting in their time counting the hours until payday, were dimly lit. A dull glow hugged their bodies like a junkie clutching the next fix.

Jason sat for minutes, maybe days, trying not to think. He was in a trance, listening to the symphony of sounds in the room.

Beep, beep, beep, exhale,

beep, beep, beep, inhale,

beep, beep, beep, exhale,

beep, beep, beep…

"Excuse me." A woman's voice sliced through his haze.

He looked up. *Can she see me?*

"Hi. How's it going?" she asked.

He stared at her trying to figure out if she was real. "Are you serious?" he finally said gesturing to his body lying on the hospital bed.

She was a little hard to see at first. But when he concentrated on her she came into focus. She was slender with long, dark hair and intense eyes. She wasn't alone.

"Are you Jason?" she asked.

He nodded suspiciously. There were three others with her.

"My name is Wendy. Your sister is dating my brother." Her casual tone gave him the impression that this was all very normal.

"Your family asked me to come and visit you," she said.

All the thoughts that he was trying to drown out with his trance came rushing back. "I don't know what's happening," Jason said sounding panicked.

She came closer and kneeled beside him.

"You're in a coma."

He stared at his body remembering snippets of the dismal things the medical people had said.

"I'm here to help you," Wendy said. "Well, actually, I'm not really the one who can help you, but my companions are." She moved toward them and they came into focus.

The first was an impressive-looking Indian woman who strongly resembled Wendy. She had a thick stripe of black paint over her eyes; it came to a point at the tip of her nose. There were black-feathered wings attached to her arms, and she wore a headdress that resembled a crow or a raven. The dark beak sat in the middle of her forehead and its black glassy eyes stared down at him. He couldn't tell where the bird ended and she began.

"This is Raventalker," Wendy said. The Indian woman nodded a greeting and smiled.

"She's a gifted shaman," Wendy said, "and my ancestor."

All Jason could do was nod.

Next to Raventalker was a bald Asian man with a long braided white beard. He was wearing golden robes. He appeared both young and old, and as if he was about to laugh at any moment.

"This is Li Ming," Wendy said. Li Ming gave Jason a little wave and a smile. "He re-patterns and weaves damaged energy."

The third companion was not human.

Wendy must have noticed Jason's confusion when he looked at this strange entity.

"And this is Oshira. She's never been human."

Oshira's body looked like iridescent rays of white, violet, blue and pink light that shimmered and shifted. Jason could see within her form the outline of a flowing gown and long wavy hair. Her features weren't constant, but she was beautiful. She felt beautiful.

"Man, this is one messed-up dream," Jason said. "What the fuck is going on?"

"The cavalry has arrived," Wendy proclaimed, making a sweeping gesture with her arm like Vanna White.

Can this get any stranger?

"Jason," Wendy said, "these are my Spirit Helpers. They're very wise and powerful healers. They can help you through this if you want. But it's your decision."

"I think it's too late," Jason told them, his tone defeated.

"Maybe… maybe not," Wendy said.

"My body's too damaged. I heard the doctors talking. There's no way I can pull out of this. They're talking carrots and celery."

Wendy squinted at Jason trying to understand what he meant. "You lost me. Carrots and celery?"

"A vegetable!" Jason said through clenched teeth. "They're saying I'm gonna be a vegetable."

"Look," Wendy said, "the doctors are grasping at straws. They really don't know what's going on with you. In fact, you probably know more than they do right now."

He looked at his body, which was pale and strangely still.

"I don't want to go back in there. It's gonna be too hard."

"I've seen my Helpers work some serious magic when people want to heal," Wendy said. "You just have to say the word."

I don't want to die.

"This is so fucked up." Jason turned to the Helpers. "Let's do it."

6

From: tim@bob.com

To: lucidpath@tds.net

Sent: Sunday, March 9

Subject: the scoop

wendy,

i know dad called you this morning and asked if you could help out abby's brother jason. we're all pretty freaked out. here's what happened: last week he wasn't feeling well. had flu symptoms and felt really tired. last sunday, no one could wake him so his parents took him to the hospital. he had a high fever and his blood pressure was erratic. then by tuesday his vitals leveled out and he slipped into a deep coma. the doctors think he has a viral infection that's causing inflammation in his brain stem. the brain stem controls involuntary functions like breathing and temperature regulation. he has machines doing this for him now. they're saying that if the brain stem is damaged that he'll never be able to wake up.

abby told her mom about the shamanic stuff you do and she was really interested and kind of anxious to have you do something as soon as possible. that's why I asked dad to call you this morning.

it's really scary to think how fragile life can be. i'll try to call you tomorrow.

love, tim

2

Jason wasn't sure when he had stopped trying to make sense of all that was happening. A part of him was relieved that he wasn't alone in this freakish limbo state anymore. The thing that was most comforting at that moment was an emerging optimism that bubbled up through his panic and confusion. After who knows how many hours or days he spent staring at his pathetic body, he felt a shred of hope when Wendy and the Helpers arrived. He didn't know if the whole thing was real or not, but it was something.

The next time he looked at his hospital bed there was an Indian man standing next to it. Woven into his long black hair were several hawk feathers. He wore only a light colored animal hide loincloth and his face and muscular torso were adorned with thick stripes of red and white war paint. Next to him stood an enormous buffalo.

The Indian man began chanting and dancing around Jason's body. The singing immediately brought tears to Jason's eyes, striking some primitive emotional chord in him as he watched his own immobile form from above. He felt embarrassed to be feeling so much. Pure, unconditional love enveloped him like a warm blanket. *All these people, beings, or whatever they are, are here to help me. Why me?*

"Why *not* you?" Raventalker said as she and the others floated over to the bed.

They can read my thoughts.

Raventalker looked at him and smiled.

"I don't know if you noticed or not," Wendy explained, "but we've all been using telepathy. Even you."

A glass of water appeared in Wendy's hand and she started drinking. "Look, I can talk to you *while* drinking a glass of water!"

"You're a smartass," Jason said.

"Would you believe you're not the first person to tell me that?"

The Helpers shrank to tiny points of flying light. The lights floated over Jason's inert body and melted into it.

"They're gonna check you out," Wendy said. "See what's wrong."

This is so strange.

"I know it is," Wendy said. "A little different than getting an x-ray." She squinted and cocked her head.

"They're telling me that there's some kind of parasite or virus in you," she said. "I can see thousands of what look like tiny black bugs in your spine."

"Bugs?"

"They're talking about using salt water… saline to kill the parasite."

The Indian man started chanting loudly and dancing again.

"Who's *that* guy?" Jason asked Wendy.

"I'm guessing he's your spirit helper," she said. "I've never seen him before."

As the Indian danced, an undulating dark cloud pregnant with moisture began to form over the bed.

"It's raining in my hospital room," Jason noted incredulously.

"It's a healing rain," Wendy said. "If you think that's crazy, wait 'til you see what's coming next."

There was a low rumble and the wall behind the bed started to shake. The rumble grew thunderous. The wall broke open releasing a flood of water over the bed.

"Sea water," Wendy said.

The water rushed through Jason's body taking millions of tiny black particles with it. After the water cleared, his body coughed.

Wendy turned to Jason. "Ready?"

He knew he had to make a choice. "If I don't go back in my body, what'll happen to me?"

"Your body will die."

Jason's chest tightened. To hear her say it somehow made the possibility of death sound more real.

"Couldn't I just hang out here while those machines keep my body alive and wait until they find a cure for the virus?"

Oshira approached him. Rays of shimmering light billowed off her like gentle waves. "Your body needs you to survive."

This raised an interesting question for Jason. He looked at his body on the hospital bed and then he looked down at the version of himself that was deciding his fate.

"If that's me over there, then who am I?"

"You are Jason's dreambody," Oshira said. "The 'you' I am talking to right now is just part of your soul. The entirety of your soul, your Oversoul, decided before you were born to have this experience. You don't remember right now, but this is all part of a much bigger plan."

"That's messed up."

"I know it's hard to believe," Wendy said.

"It's hard to believe because it makes no sense," Jason said. "Why would anyone plan for something bad to happen to them?"

Oshira approached him and Jason immediately felt calm.

"This will all be made clear soon," Oshira said. "For now you have to decide if you want to live out the rest of your life as Jason or if you wish to transition fully to the world of spirit."

All of the dreams Jason had for his life swirled through his mind's eye. *My music career is just getting going. There are about three million computer games I haven't played. I want to meet an extraterrestrial and visit a crop circle. I have to figure out how to be immortal. I want to get married some day, have kids. And there's my family. I don't want to leave them. I'm not ready to go. I don't think I'll ever be ready to go.*

Jason eyed his limp, soggy body. He knew that if he went back, he wouldn't just miraculously wake up. It would take time and patience and a lot of work.

"No matter what you decide," Oshira said, "you'll be fine."

He knew she was right but he didn't know why he knew this. It wasn't logical at all. But then again there was nothing logical about any of this. One second it was a lose-lose situation, the next, a lose-probably not lose situation.

"You *are* a warrior, young one," said a deep male voice, slow and deliberate. "You still have important work to do." It was the Indian man.

When Jason looked into the man's eyes he felt a rush of heat in his chest, as if his heart was on fire.

"We'll help you," the Indian said, gesturing to the buffalo standing next to him. The massive animal approached Jason and snorted. Then it turned around and ran full speed toward the hospital bed. It leaped into the air and dove into Jason's body as if it were a lake.

I need to go back. Jason floated over to his body and slipped in.

3

Arizona…

The beeping of the heart monitor sped up. Jason opened his eyes, but no one had seen it happen.

4

After Jason re-entered his body, he could only stay in it for short periods of time. He felt like a stranger inside. There was almost something perverse about being in it, like he was taking advantage of its vulnerability. But he knew it was important to keep trying; to get used to how dense and unresponsive his body felt in this state. He kept telling himself, "I'm allowed to be here." But he wanted his body's consent – some kind of response. Anything. A sigh. A raised finger. A toe wiggle. Some sign that his body was still in this with him.

While waiting for a sign, Jason had an enjoyable dip in the sea of his anxieties. And the water was mighty cold. His biggest fear: *What if this is it? What if, for the rest of eternity, I'm going to be stuck in this "not alive, not dead" state?* His thoughts picked up speed. *What exactly is eternity? Is it a human concept? After all, time is a human concept. It doesn't really exist. And since eternity falls into the "time" category, maybe eternity doesn't really exist either. But then again, if it does exist, would that be a good thing, especially if this is how things are going to be? Am I pro-eternity or anti-eternity?* He had never thought about that before.

He was caught in a riptide of distress. *Maybe I'm dreaming. Maybe I'm already dead. Maybe I never existed. What part of me is thinking all of this?* His thoughts tossed him around in the confined space of his body until he didn't know anything.

Jason's stream of consciousness quickly swelled into a tsunami as he was introduced to a new sensation: paranoia. He was being watched. On the other side of the darkness he could feel someone's eyes on him.

"Who's there?" Jason asked.

Nothing.

"Come on. I know someone's there."

Silence.

"You're freakin' me out."

Out of the darkness flew a circular white object, which landed at his feet. It was a life preserver with the initials S.O.S. printed on it in red.

Following it came the buffalo. Jason felt completely lost.

"You were in pretty deep," the buffalo said with a Scottish accent.

Jason was clueless.

"I didn't want you to drown in your worries," the buffalo clarified. "Get it?"

"Oh," Jason replied.

"Just trying to lighten things up a bit."

"Is everyone in coma land a smartass?" Jason asked.

"That offends me," the buffalo said. "I'm not an ass. I'm a buffalo. My name is Bill."

"Buffalo Bill?"

"Yes," he said. His chest swelled with pride. "I am Buffalo Bill."

Maybe I've gone insane. Jason hadn't considered that option.

"You don't remember me?" Bill asked.

"No."

"I used to visit you when you were shorter," he said.

Jason saw an image of himself talking with Bill when he was about two-years-old.

"I'm here to help you get better. I have been given great gifts of healing."

"How do you do that?" Jason asked.

"I don't know. It just happens."

Bill stepped closer and looked into his eyes. "Where is your trust? I don't see it anywhere."

"Trust in what?" he asked.

"A flower never wonders if it will bloom."

And with that Bill vanished.

From: tim@bob.com

To: lucidpath@tds.net

Sent: Saturday, March 15

Subject: baby steps

hey wen,

jason's been opening his eyes – last night he looked right at abby like he recognized her. she's been tickling his chin trying to annoy him so he'll wake up. after about ten seconds he moves his chin in this funny way. the doctors say we have to distinguish between voluntary and involuntary movements. abby thinks he's moving his chin voluntarily. it looks like it to me too.

never thought I'd get excited about someone opening their eyes and moving their chin.

later, tim

5

Jason watched his family keep vigil over him. Friends and relatives streamed in and out of his hospital room. He could feel their shock and their prayers. He was happy that so many people cared, but he also found it sad. As much as Jason liked attention, he didn't like that he was the cause of all this distress.

"Hi Jason," said a familiar voice. He couldn't remember her name, but he was relieved to see her.

"How are you doing?" she asked.

"I don't know. I guess a little better," said Jason. "I've been in and out of my body. I can't stay in it for too long. It feels claustrophobic."

"I'll bet," she said.

"I hate doing this to my family," he said.

"It's a shitty situation, I know, but certainly an opportunity for growth for everyone involved."

"How the hell does my being in a coma lead to my family's growth?"

"Going through a crisis pushes you into new emotional territory. It puts spiritual hair on your chest."

"Nice spin."

The conversation with her was a little too normal. He found it disconcerting.

"Who are you again?" he asked.

"Wendy. Your sister is dating my little brother."

"How did you end up here?"

"Your family asked me to – "

"No, no. I mean… literally… how did you get here?"

She closed her eyes. "Listen," she said.

He didn't hear anything.

"No, behind me."

He heard a faint monotonous pounding sound.

"You hear the drum?" she asked.

"Yeah," he said with surprise, "I think I do."

"That's how I got here. I just followed the sound until I found you."

"Where's the drumming coming from?"

"New Jersey."

"Of course… New Jersey," Jason said. "Do you think a large straitjacket would do the trick?"

"I think they're one-size-fits-all."

"That's not helpful."

Wendy grinned. "Yeah, I know. Right now," she explained, "my body is lying on my bed in my house, which unfortunately happens to be in New Jersey."

"You're a real person?"

She smiled. "Nutty, isn't it?"

He let out a nervous laugh.

"I know talking to me like this is a little on the strange side," she said, "but it's a really ancient practice."

Wendy explained how medicine men and women from cultures all over the planet have been going into trance and establishing relationships with powerful helping spirits for tens of thousands of years. She said that, when invited, these spirits can offer guidance and healing.

"It's like I'm dreaming while I'm awake. Basically all I'm doing is creating a bridge with my consciousness between the dreamtime, where we are right now, and physical reality, where you're in a hospital in Arizona and I'm in a trance in New Jersey."

"So this is a dream. It's not real," he said.

"Actually," Wendy suggested, "it's highly possible that physical reality is an illusion. The more time I spend in the dreamtime, the more I realize that reality is... well, it's complicated. There are lots of layers to it. The physical reality we're all so attached to is not all there is. There seems to be a lot of realities existing at the same time. So what's real to you at any given moment just depends on what layer you're paying attention to. Make sense?"

He nodded, but felt overwhelmed and disturbed. Jason wondered if Wendy knew that he'd been wrestling with understanding the nature of reality since he was a kid. Did she know that he'd spent many sleepless and anxiety-filled nights trying to wrap his brain around what was real and what wasn't? Did she know that what he was experiencing right now, being in a coma, not knowing if he existed, was the source of countless nightmares and panic attacks he'd had since he was little – that he was now *living* his nightmare?

"I don't know what's real anymore. It's one thing to wax poetic about reality in a philosophy class, but actually spending extended periods of time in this limbo hell state is… I don't have words to describe how fucked up it is."

Wendy's eyes softened. "I can't imagine what you're going through."

Jason looked at his body and shook his head. "I wouldn't wish this on anyone."

A large shadow caught Wendy's eye. Out of the darkness the buffalo appeared.

Buffalo Bill stood in front of Wendy and looked deeply into her eyes. He was examining the shape of her soul. Wendy realized that he was checking her out and relaxed into his gaze, allowing him access.

After several intense moments, Bill stepped back and snorted.

"She's for real," he said to Jason.

Wendy smiled. "That's a relief!"

Buffalo Bill addressed her. "Show Jason how you came to be a dreamwalker."

"Dreamwalker?" she asked.

"A shaman," he said.

"I'm not a shaman."

Bill's expression oozed impatience. "You walk between the worlds to serve others, am I right?"

"Yeah, that pretty much sums it up," she responded.

"Well then, show Jason how you were called to be a dreamwalker. It'll help him understand who you are."

"Sure, if you think it'll help."

The darkness surrounding them shimmered like the surface of a rippling pond as a scene from Wendy's past appeared in front of them.

A large rustic-looking room came into focus like a hologram. Wendy was sitting in a circle of about thirty people. On the floor in the center of the room was a make-shift altar filled with a menagerie of sacred objects. Everyone's attention was on the teacher who spoke animatedly to the group.

"It began about three years ago," Wendy said, narrating over this vision. "My husband had enrolled me in a week-long shamanic training program for my birthday that year.

"Everything I learned that week... about the different aspects of the soul... about healing and the nature of reality... it was like all the pieces came together for me. But then there was the night that changed everything."

Wendy explained that the evening before the program ended, the instructor had invited the group to participate in a healing ceremony.

"The teacher asked for a volunteer to help him and before he could even finish the sentence my hand was up in the air. I didn't know what I was volunteering for."

The meeting room that night was dark except for the glow of a candle that was sitting on the altar. The students stood in a wide circle, holding frame drums and rattles. A woman in her fifties, battling a chronic illness, volunteered to receive healing. She lay on a blanket on the floor next to the altar. The teacher kneeled on one side of the woman and Wendy on the other.

The group began to drum and rattle a monotonous, rapid rhythm. Wendy looked to the instructor for direction, but he just smiled at her and closed his eyes. Wendy took a deep breath and closed her eyes too. The sound of the drumming intensified. Wendy's breaths became long and deep. Her back arched slightly as if cold water ran down her spine. Her head rolled to the side and then fell forward. Two more surges shot up her spine. The second one was more powerful. Her eyes opened and rolled upward. She grit her teeth and her breaths came in heaves.

The teacher leaned forward over the ill woman and cupped his hands over her stomach. He blew three times into the hole his hands had made, before receding into the background.

The spirit of Raventalker materialized behind Wendy. Raventalker quickly appraised the situation before slipping into Wendy's body. In response, Wendy's body shook with power as if she had a strong chill. Her fingers curled against her thighs like talons and shiny black wings spread from her back while her head and neck made subtle bird-like movements.

Raventalker's face, with its mask of black eye paint, was superimposed over Wendy's face. Wendy's eyes opened suddenly, only she was no longer Wendy. Her eyes darted to the right as she surveyed the people drumming and rattling. She smiled mischievously.

Raventalker examined the woman lying in front of her. She ran her hand over the woman's body stopping at her solar plexus. Like a bird, Raventalker cocked her head to the right and then jutted her face forward as if she had just discovered something interesting in the woman's body.

The ill woman's solar plexus started to vibrate like static. The fuzzy energy transformed into a bubbling puddle of putrid, mustard-colored fluid. Out of the fluid emerged hundreds of slithering maggots.

Raventalker grabbed a bowl of water that was sitting on the edge of the altar and placed it on the floor next to her. She deftly reached into the writhing pile of maggots, grabbed a handful, and then deposited them into the water. Raventalker continued extracting the maggots until they were gone. When she finished, the ill woman's solar plexus was a spinning disk of yellow light.

As the drumming slowed, Raventalker slipped out of Wendy's body and disappeared into the shadows. Wendy's body relaxed and her eye's popped open. She looked sheepishly around the room at the stunned faces of her colleagues.

Buffalo Bill and Jason shifted their attention back to Wendy as the scene faded from view.

"After that night," Wendy said, "I knew my life would never be the same again."

"And here you are," Buffalo Bill said with a smile.

"And here I am," she replied.

"What's it like to have your body taken over like that?" Jason asked.

"It's unnerving. And I feel a little used. No dinner... no foot rub... nothing. She just waltzes right in and makes herself at home."

Buffalo Bill squinted at Wendy and then addressed Jason. "And you say *I'm* a smartass."

"The whole process definitely took some getting used to. When I relax into it, my Wendy-ness kind of takes a back seat and watches everything. That night, when it first happened, I didn't really know Raventalker. I'd just met her earlier that week during the training. But she was strangely familiar. I trusted her immediately."

Buffalo Bill smirked at Jason in response to Wendy's last statement. Jason smiled and rolled his eyes.

"I'd better get going," Wendy said. "I'm late for work. I'll be back."

Before he could reply, she was gone.

"Must be nice to be able to come and go like that," Jason said.

Jason's whole being was keyed up with the kind of tension that builds in anticipation of something really good, something really big. He also felt like he wanted to throw up.

6

J ason slipped back into the stiff darkness of his body. His lungs, heavy and thick with fluid, begged for some elbowroom. His body convulsed with silent coughs as it tried to clear the fluid. *I'm drowning.* His pulse raced and his breathing was rapid and shallow. Panic contorted his face. He had to get out.

Jason's dreambody slipped out of his body and retreated to his usual chair at the foot of the bed. He noticed water on the floor. It was about six inches deep.

He watched as the doctors talked to his parents about pneumonia and infection with great concern. He heard bits and pieces, "situation is worrisome… immune system isn't strong enough… may not make it through the night."

The water on the floor was now two feet deep and rising. The heart monitor beeped faster as if in response.

Jason stared at the water and wondered how long it would take for his body to drown. *Maybe I'm not meant to live through this. Maybe I wasn't supposed to survive this long.* Jason imagined the line on the heart monitor going flat. No more beeping, just a single tone.

I can't handle this, he thought; the familiar sea of panic churned inside of him. *I can't die like this.*

He heard something in the distance. Faint drums. *Wendy's coming.* He held on, counting on her to fix the situation.

"Ever hear this one?" Wendy said as she came into focus. "Two cannibals were eating a clown. One says to the other, 'Does this taste funny to you?'"

Jason looked at her as if she were speaking Chinese.

"Does this taste funny to you?" she repeated. "Get it? Cannibals eating a clown? Clowns are funny?"

"First, maybe if I wasn't dying I'd find your joke funny," Jason said. "Second, I fucking hate clowns."

"Got it," she said, her expression changing to one of mock seriousness. "No clowns." She looked down and asked, "Where'd the water come from?"

"I'm not sure," Jason said. "I heard them say something about pneumonia."

"Maybe the water represents fluid in your lungs," Wendy suggested.

"They say I won't make it through the night."

Wendy's Helpers quickly assessed the situation and went to work. Raventalker sang an unearthly melody as she swept her feathered arms over Jason's body. At times her voice sounded like a flute and at other times, like a bird.

Li Ming was at the head of the bed maneuvering his hands above Jason's forehead like a magician, his ageless face intently focused and calm. Thin bands of golden light came out of Li Ming's palms and illuminated Jason's face.

The rays of Oshira's luminescent body brightened and swirled in the middle of the room. A deep tone reminiscent of the rich timbre of a Tibetan singing bowl rose out of her body and seemed to take shape in front of her. Using the sound she produced a crystal staff made of brilliant white light. With the staff she traced a two-foot square on the floor of the hospital room. The square fell away, leaving a hole, which allowed the water that filled the room to quickly empty.

"Thanks," Jason said. "That water was making me nervous."

"Your body is fighting a bad infection," Raventalker said, "but the worst is over."

"You're gonna be okay," Wendy reassured him. "I know it's hard, but try not to listen to the doctors."

"It's strange. Just a little while ago I was completely freaked out. Now I feel strangely calm." Jason looked at the Helpers and smiled. "You're good!"

Raventalker pointed at Jason. "Remember to laugh," she threatened.

"I know. I know," he said. "Eat a clown."

Wendy and the Helpers disappeared.

Jason was renewed. "We're going to pull through this," he told his body. He went back into his body and noticed a difference right away. It felt more spacious. He had room to breathe.

From: tim@bob.com

To: lucidpath@tds.net

Sent: Wednesday, April 02

Subject: jason

wendy,

jason spent eight hours off the ventilator today! he's breathing on his own which means that his brains stem is better (something the docs originally thought was damaged). abby told me that he has been responding to pain in his feet. a new development. i guess a nurse was trying to draw blood and she said jason was pulling strongly away in "anticipation" – she hadn't pricked him yet. good signs. i'm just gonna keep repeating in my head "jason can make it happen." we'll see.

peace out sista – tim

p.s. how about that iraqi war thing everybody's talking about, nutty.

7

Jason relaxed into the space of his body. He thought about being outdoors and feeling the sun. He remembered a walk that he had taken in the desert days before he got sick. He lost himself in the memory. He recalled the black shirt he wore that day thinking that the temperature was going to be cool, but it had gotten pretty hot. *That's the thing about winter in the desert, it can be a frosty sixty degrees one minute, requiring long underwear and a down jacket, and the next minute, you're ripping off your clothes, seeing mirages and babbling incoherently to yourself. Kind of like I'm doing right now.*

The cloudless sky that day had been huge and Easter egg blue. Jason wanted to be where he couldn't see any signs of civilization. No rooftops, telephone wires, no streets. He didn't want to hear any traffic. It was just him and the desert. He was on the surface of Mars. A space explorer looking for signs of alien life on a barren planet...

"Your son never had pneumonia," a doctor was telling Jason's parents back in the hospital room. "He had some heavy mucus plugs, which we were able to suction out."

Jason flew out of his body. *The healing worked!*

"But," the doctor continued, "he may have experienced irreversible damage... cerebral hemisphere... never wake up... vegetative state."

"No, no, no," Jason screamed at the doctors. "You fuckers don't know what you're talking about. *I am not* a vegetable. I refuse to be a vegetable ! Vegetables suck. *You* suck. Fucking prick !" He stopped his rant, fear rising above the anger.

What if they're right? What if –

"That's enough young warrior." The Indian guide appeared. He was firm, but gentle. "You're carrying on as if your hair's on fire."

"Did you hear what that asshole said? He said I'm done. That's it. No more. Dead. Done."

Buffalo Bill appeared behind Jason and asked, "Would you like fries with your coffin?"

Jason resisted smiling. He sat down and put his head in his hands. *I'm losing it.*

"I don't want to die," Jason said. "But I can't do this anymore."

"Humans these days give too much power to other humans," the Indian said. "This is a dangerous thing."

"What do you mean?"

"Among my people it was known that there are other forces at work in the universe. If you were sick you would visit the medicine maker and she would commune with these forces to help you heal."

"Forces? What forces?" asked Jason.

"The spirit of the wind, the sea, the rocks and trees, the heavens." He gestured to the doctor who was talking to Jason's parents. "The medicine makers of today have lost touch with these forces. To heal someone is a big job for a mere human."

"Yeah, but look at all the advances we've made," Jason said. "Modern medicine has helped millions of people live long lives."

"Is the goal of being human to live a long life?" the Indian asked.

His words hit Jason in the face like cold water. "It's *my* goal," Jason whispered.

"What's driving your desire to get well, warrior friend," the Indian asked, "your fear of death or your love of life?"

"I'm afraid to die," Jason admitted, looking at his inert body. "But I'm afraid to live like that. Either way I'm a prisoner."

"Death is a prison?"

"Who knows, but I'm in no hurry to find out."

Jason was restless. He always felt edgy when he thought about death. And he thought about death a lot. But now he couldn't escape the subject. He had nowhere to go. Nothing to distract him. Every time he looked at his body he thought about death. It was everywhere.

"You don't look so good," Wendy said, catching Jason by surprise.

"I didn't hear the drums."

"You were really hard to find this time," she said. "What's going on?"

"Things are looking a little grim," Jason said, gesturing to his body on the bed.

"He's been listening to the sour words of the medicine person," the Indian said.

"They obviously don't realize that you can hear them," Wendy said. "And it's probably impossible for you not to listen."

"I'm sick of listening. I'm sick of thinking," Jason said. "I wish I could turn everything off."

"But then you'd be dead," Buffalo Bill said. "Or would you?"

"Great," Jason said. "Another serving of smartass from the buffalo."

"You know that offends me," Bill said.

"I don't give a sh– "

Jason was distracted by a pinpoint of brilliant white light that appeared by the ceiling. The light expanded like liquid flower petals. A lotus. It was the brightest light Jason had ever seen, but it didn't hurt his eyes.

"Fasten your seatbelts," Wendy said.

An amorphous being descended from the center of the lotus star and floated above Jason. The entity was hard to define. It seemed more male than female, but it was difficult to tell at first. It was wearing flowing robes. If you looked closely you could catch traces of his features in the shimmering light. Long, wavy hair. Sunken cheeks. Piercing gray and gold eyes. He looked like the archetypal Wise Man.

The Wise Man's eyes met Jason's and everything stopped. Jason was locked in an invisible embrace until he lost all sense of himself, as if they were one entity. Jason managed to pull his awareness out a bit from the experience and noticed a familiar feeling. He felt a complete absence of tension. It was as if every particle of his essence had been set free, released from the dense burden of the physical world. He was home.

As Jason melted into this experience he noticed the most pleasing and unusual sounds. Musical tones unlike anything he'd ever heard enveloped Jason like ribbons of silk. The Wise Man was communicating with him.

All at once Jason understood. He knew that what he was going through was no accident. He was in a coma because he needed the experience to help him face his paralyzing fear of death. To fulfill his soul's purpose he needed to break through the bonds of fear that were keeping him from developing to his full potential. Until he faced his fear, he would be trapped in its cocoon. At that moment he understood that the coma was not an unexpected guest... but he himself had sent the invitation.

There was a sudden shift. The beautiful tones swirled faster and faster and the essence of Jason's being seemed to vibrate in response. He was building momentum like a spinning top until there was a pop. And then silence. His awareness floated in darkness, but he wasn't afraid. He still felt the comforting embrace of the mysterious Wise Man. The haunting music drifted around him again like a gentle, steady stream.

He was shown the beginning – the birth of his existence. It began with an intention, a desire to experience and to evolve. This desire gave rise to a faint awareness – that he could separate from all that is and exist as an independent being, a soul. The awareness and desire fed off each other, growing stronger until the primordial particles of his soul gathered and burst out of the heavens like a shooting star.

His newborn soul was cared for by the Old Ones – a group of highly evolved souls whose job it was to nurture infant souls – until he was ready for his first experience. Jason saw pieces of his soul splinter and travel to many places and lead many lives, each one returning home pregnant with every kind of experience possible. He saw his soul take shape lifetime after lifetime – changing color as it matured, becoming brighter. He knew that "Jason" was one of the many experiences his soul was having and that no matter what happened, "Jason" would be fine.

He saw that his soul would continue on this journey until its evolution was complete. When that time came he would explode in a flash of brilliant light, the particles of his essence becoming one with everything – once again.

The Wise Man released Jason from his gaze and, like iridescent swirls of liquid smoke, began to melt back into the center of the lotus until he was gone.

Jason appeared to be in a deep trance.

"Man," Jason whispered.

"Intense?" Wendy asked.

"I don't have words to describe it. Everything makes so much sense. I've died hundreds of times. I don't have to be afraid."

Wendy nodded solemnly and then broke into a smile.

From: tim@bob.com

To: lucidpath@tds.net

Sent: Wednesday, April 05

Subject: Re: jason

we're all completely blown away by your last meeting with jason. carol, jason and abby's mom, figured out that at the same time the wise man was with him, jason was pretty much at death's door. abby and i hadn't gotten to the hospital yet, but the doctors were preparing everyone – saying he wouldn't make it through the night. he had too much fluid in his lungs and was drowning. he surprised everyone and pulled through. amazing!

abby was telling me that ever since jason was little he has been petrified of death. she can remember all of the family having to have these conversations with him about it. even when he was as young as four years old. cryogenics is a huge interest of his. he has always wanted to freeze his body – so he can be somewhat eternal. abby said that when you first contacted jason, there was no doubt in her mind that if jason had a choice in the matter – he was choosing life. she thinks it would be because of this very well-developed fear of death. she thought you might want to know this so maybe you can talk to him about it the next time you see him.

i'll try to call you this weekend – tim

8

Jason heard the drums this time and waited for Wendy to appear. He was looking forward to seeing her. His memory of the experience with the Wise Man was fading fast, but he felt like the whole thing had spun him in a new direction.

He looked to the corner of the room where she usually appeared and soon saw her faint image. She was alone.

"Hi," Jason said.

"Hey," Wendy said. "You look so much better today."

"I've had a lot to think about since the Wise Man was here."

Wendy was silent for a moment. Then she looked up and looked him right in the eye.

"So the word on the street is that you have a pretty big fear of death," Wendy said.

"Big's an understatement. I've been terrified of it since I was little."

Jason remembered violent scenes he'd seen in movies and on TV, of people dying in horrible ways. There was one scene that stayed with him. It was a car accident where the mangled bloody body of the driver was hanging out of the car where the door used to be. He didn't know if it was something he had seen in person or in a movie, but the look on the victim's face had kept him awake more times than he could count. He could see the person's eyes: frozen with fear, but vacant. Jason shuddered with the familiar feeling of panic.

"How'd you know about my fear of death?"

"Your sister. I've been e-mailing updates to my brother every time I visit you and I guess he forwards the e-mails to your family. I don't know how much they believe in what I'm doing, but they haven't asked me to stop yet.

"In fact, I was thinking that it'd be cool if you could give me a message to pass on to your family so that they'll know that I'm really talking to you. It might be a way for them to validate our interaction. So why don't you give me some information about you that only your parents would know."

At that instant, Wendy, whose body was back in New Jersey, received a quick succession of information. She felt a strong physical sensation: her heart fluttered and then skipped a beat. It was all very strange.

This was followed by an intense feeling of panic, of being trapped and unable to breathe. Wendy knew it was an anxiety attack.

Then she saw an image of strawberries and Jason's mom, and noticed that he was smiling about this.

And the phrase "quantum mind" popped into her mind.

But the phrase didn't stick. Coming out of the trance Wendy repeated the information over and over to herself so she wouldn't forget it. *Heart flutter, anxiety attack, strawberries, mom, quantum… something. What did he say? It wasn't quantum physics or mechanics. It was something simple… Great, I can't remember two words I heard three minutes ago, but I can remember the chemical formula for glucose from my high school chemistry class. Damn, my brain.*

From: tim@bob.com
To: lucidpath@tds.net
Sent: Monday, April 07
Subject: Re: hello

here's what jason and abby's mom wrote in response to your latest journey

tim

------- Original Message -------

From: mom and dad
To: tim@bob.com
Sent: Sunday, April 06
Subject: wendy's journey

Abby,

I think Wendy's journeys are very interesting and I believe she has a connection with Jason at this time. The heart flutter I think could be referring to his T-Wave Inversion. We found out about the t wave when he was around fifteen years old. When he was admitted to the hospital last month the doctors were concerned that something was wrong with his heart until I told them about the T wave. Since then they have not been so concerned because that's just Jason. As you know, since he was about four years old he's had an unusual fear of death. He used to cry and cry that someday he was going to die. Nothing seemed to ease his fear. You know Jason wanted to freeze his head if he ever died so that he could come back when a cure was found. I feel like in a way he kind of froze his head now and is trying to come back. I don't know exactly what he's referring to by Quantum Leap - but we used to watch that show. Strawberries? You know he likes my strawberry shortcake. I'm glad that Wendy is not so concerned with permanent brain damage and that the healers are working on his brain to help him heal. That gives me peace of mind because it is one of my main fears. Maybe now that Jason has faced his immortality he can leave this fear and start focusing on healing.

I love you, Mom

9

Jason felt someone gently stroking his head. He heard a familiar quiet voice. It was his mom. He focused hard so he could hear what she was saying.

"I got your messages Jay," his mom whispered. "I know you're scared, but you're not going to die. You're way too strong.

"When you wake up I'm gonna make you strawberry shortcake for breakfast, lunch, and dinner." She paused and then he heard her say, "I had no idea you liked that show *Quantum Leap* so much. You were pretty little when we watched that."

Quantum Leap? Jason rolled his eyes. *That's not what I said.*

10

J ason thought he saw something dart across the hospital room. Maybe a bird? It was tiny and quick.

He had been out of his body for a while now because while in it, it was getting harder and harder to breathe. When he was free from the confines of his form, he found that his hospital room was filling with water again: not a good sign.

He heard Wendy's drum in the distance. Her theme song. He thought about how cool it would be if everyone had a theme song that would play every time you entered a room or a building. And you could change the song depending on what mood you were in. If you were having a bad day you could program Darth Vader's theme song to play as you walked into the grocery store. Or if you were feeling obnoxious you could arrange for Wayne Newton's *Danke Schoene* to play in the waiting room at your dentist's office. It'd be like hosting your own variety show.

"Hey Jason," Wendy said as she appeared.

The Helpers were with her and they quickly set to work draining the water from the room. Four hummingbirds buzzed around Jason's body. They stuck their beaks in his chest and started sucking out the fluid that filled his lungs.

There are birds sucking mucous out of my lungs.

"How are you doing?" Wendy asked.

"Well," Jason said, "nothing makes sense. I don't like being in my body but I feel weird being out of it. I think about everything too much and I'm really confused. Oh yeah, and small birds have impaled my chest."

"If I start thinking that this… you, them," he gestured to the Helpers, "is real, then I think I might lose what's left of my mind. That is, the parts that haven't turned to oatmeal yet. So I've decided to write it all off as some crazy dream I'm having. A dream makes sense. You being real doesn't."

Jason noticed that Wendy looked concerned.

"I know I'm really sick," Jason said. "I think my mind is creating all of this because I'm sick. Like when you have a high fever and hallucinate."

"You know," Wendy said, "when it comes down to it I don't think it really matters how you make sense of all this. I mean as long as you focus on doing what you have to do to get better. It doesn't matter how you get there."

"You've gotta admit though," he said looking at the hummingbirds, "this is some crazy shit!"

Wendy smiled, "Maybe I'll write a book about it some day."

"Nobody'd believe it."

"Yeah, you're probably right."

"By the way," Jason said, "you screwed up the message."

Wendy was confused. "What message?"

"I didn't say quantum leap. I said quantum mind."

"Shit, you're right," she said. "That's what it was. You gave me so much so quickly that the phrase slipped away from me. Sorry about that."

"You know, it's stuff like that that really messes me up," Jason said.

"What do you mean?"

"If I'm making all of this up, how did my mom know what I told you?"

"Gosh, I don't know. Maybe you pulled off some kind of crazy quantum leap thing, Scott Bakula-style," Wendy said with a smile. "Or hey, I have an idea. Maybe it was the e-mail I sent your family letting them know what you told me. Yeah, it could've been the e-mail."

Raventalker floated toward them. Her dark eyes set on Jason. "Your body's in limbo…" she said, "…because your doubt is giving it mixed messages."

Jason gave her a quizzical look.

"The longer you're unclear," Raventalker said, "the longer you'll be in this in-between state. Your body will eventually break down and make the decision for you."

Jason stared at his body, his expression frozen.

"Hang in there Jason," Wendy said.

"Remember what the Wise Man showed you," Raventalker chimed in. "No matter what happens, you'll get through this." Jason didn't take his eyes off his body as Wendy and Raventalker vanished from the room.

11

New Jersey...

Wendy remembered the phrase this time. Quantum mind. She'd never heard it before, which was why she figured it was so easy to forget. She was at a loss for what it meant... if it meant anything at all.

Out of curiosity she plugged the phrase into Google and was shocked to find over 600,000 matches. Her heart sped up.

The first result took her to a website for the University of Arizona's "Quantum Mind" division.

The U of A has a Quantum Mind division? This can't be a coincidence.

It was strange. It felt personal, a little too close to home. She had received her bachelor's degree from the University of Arizona.

Within seconds she discovered that "Quantum Mind" was an actual science that examines the link between quantum physics and consciousness.

Consciousness? A coma certainly falls into that category. Wendy's subatomic particles buzzed with excitement. *How did Jason know about this?*

She looked at another result. The second website belonged to an Oregon couple, Arny and Amy Mindell, both authors. Arny's book, *Quantum Mind: The Edge between Physics and Psychology* popped up on the screen.

Wendy read the description: "What do your disconnected parts have in common? Is the universe dreaming us or are we dreaming the universe? Mindell takes you into physics, psychology, and shamanism – on a transformative journey into the depth of experience."

A chill spilled down her spine like cold water. *This is amazing. I can't believe I've never heard of this book.*

The buzzing in her body was almost audible. She scrolled down the page on the Mindells' website and stopped short when saw another book, this one written by Amy Mindell.

"Holy shit," Wendy whispered.

It was called *Coma: A Healing Journey* and was designed to teach family members and medical staff how to communicate with comatose patients.

From: tim@bob.com

To: lucidpath@tds.net

Sent: Wednesday, April 09

Subject: good news

what's up?

abby's mom just called and said that jason seems more awake than ever tonight. but she said he seems scared - really frightened. and he keeps checking out his vent. she said that she was trying to tell him what's happening to him in a comforting way, but he still seemed scared. i don't blame him. abby was wondering if jason knows that we're there with him? she doesn't want him to feel alone in all this.

abby also told me that when she went to see jason earlier today, she asked him, "does quantum mind mean something to you?" she told him to move his head off the pillow if it does and sure enough he did! she said it was plain as day. she's e-mailing anyone and everyone with a connection to quantum mind to try to get help for jason. she already ordered the quantum mind book and that coma book that you found.

pretty exciting stuff!

tim

12

Jason was in his body when Wendy and the Helpers arrived. There was water in the room again. This time it came up to Wendy's knees.

For the first time, Jason's usually prone body was propped upright in the hospital bed. His face was contorted with panic. He looked like the model for Edward Munch's painting *The Scream*. Wendy went over to him and whispered in his ear.

"Jason, it's Wendy. I want you to reach deep down inside to the part of yourself that knows how to wake up." Her words were like fireflies spiraling into the depths of Jason's consciousness.

"You can do this with ease if you want," she continued. "You know how to wake up. There's nothing to be afraid of. You're not alone. We're here to help you."

Oshira emptied the water from the room while Raventalker chanted and danced around Jason. Li Ming placed glowing amber crystals on Jason's temples.

Raventalker placed her hands on Wendy's head and together they melted deep into Jason. They found themselves in a dark, disorienting place. The walls of darkness felt close, like they were in a small cave. Raventalker clapped her hands once and a dim golden light appeared.

"That was cool," Wendy said.

Raventalker clapped two times and the light was gone.

"You try it," Raventalker suggested.

Wendy clapped once and the light came back on. "You should market that," she told Raventalker.

"Go away," a small, frightened voice whispered. "Go away. Please go away. You're not real."

Raventalker and Wendy turned and saw a little boy, about six, curled up in a ball on the ground. His head was tucked under his arms as if the sky was about to fall on him. It was Jason.

"It's okay, Jason," Wendy said as she went over to him. "We're not going to hurt you. What a scary place this is."

Wendy closed her eyes and put out a mental call to Mama, the spirit of an Inuit woman who worked with lost and frightened soul parts.

"I'm here," Mama said tenderly. Her short, thick body was wrapped in a long dress of animal skins the color of buttermilk. She wore her white hair in two braids and her face was scrunched into a wide, toothless smile.

Mama went to little Jason and put her arms around him and rocked. She sang a soft lullaby.

By the end of her song Jason was in Mama's lap.

"Do you like magic, little one?" Mama asked.

Jason looked up at her and nodded.

"I'm going to show you some magic."

Mama closed her eyes and smiled. Within seconds the gloomy cave turned into a cozy log cabin warmed by firelight and bear skin rugs.

"How'd you do that?" Jason asked.

"With wishes," Mama said. "This place can be whatever you want it to be. Go ahead and try it. Start with something simple… like a tree. Close your eyes and think of a beautiful tree. Imagine climbing this tree and whispering in its ear. What does the tree say?"

When Jason opened his eyes he found that a magnificent oak tree had sprouted in the middle of the cabin.

"You did that," little Jason said. "It's a trick."

Mama laughed. "Oh, you think so, eh? Try it yourself. Just make a wish and then imagine how you'll feel when it comes true."

Jason closed his eyes and concentrated.

When he opened his eyes he was surrounded by the towering figures of Spiderman, Wolverine, a red and a blue Power Ranger, and the alien from the movie *ET*.

"It worked!" Jason cried. He jumped out of Mama's lap and ran over to them. "They're here to protect me," he announced with pride.

"Protect you from what, little one?"

Little Jason bit his lower lip and looked at the floor. He seemed afraid to say it out loud.

"It's okay," Mama said. He looked up at her with wide eyes. She gave him an encouraging nod.

With a whisper Jason said, "Dying."

Mama's eyes filled with compassion. "I see," she said. "You're afraid to die?"

The boy nodded.

"Is that how you ended up in this place?"

He nodded again and then explained.

"I saw something bad." His eyes glazed over with the memory.

"You can show me if you like."

Little Jason shrugged, and squeezed his eyes shut as if trying to erase the image from his mind.

"Sometimes sharing an upsetting experience with someone else can make you feel better," she told him.

The boy shrugged again, and let out a big sigh. "Okay," he mumbled, "I guess so."

Mama opened her arms and Little Jason crawled back into her lap, resting his head against her shoulder.

The air in front of them buzzed and blurred like a TV station with bad reception. An image of a light blue 1960s-era sedan flashed on an invisible screen. The driver's side of the vehicle was mangled and twisted. A middle-aged man's torso dangled upside down from the driver's seat where the car door had been. The front of the man's crisp white button-down shirt was covered with blood, and his lifeless hazel eyes stared blankly into the distance.

Suddenly, the perspective shifted abruptly and they were viewing the accident from above. The details of the smoking wreck and its driver swiftly receded and faded away.

"Oh my," Mama said squeezing him tightly. "What a terrible thing to see."

Jason nodded. "And then I had scary dreams that something bad was going to happen to me, too."

Mama gently stroked his head. "That does sound scary." She lifted his chin so that he was looking into her eyes. "But death is nothing to be frightened of, little one. When your body dies your spirit goes home. And when you get there everyone throws a big party in your honor!"

"Like a birthday party?" Jason asked.

"Better than a birthday party! All your spirit friends welcome you home and celebrate how brave you were when you were alive."

Little Jason smiled.

"That doesn't sound very scary, does it?"

Jason shook his head.

Wendy bowed slightly to Mama. "Thank you," she said.

Mama gummed a smile and disappeared.

Wendy and Raventalker reappeared outside Jason's body where they were greeted by a serene stillness.

"This is very good," Raventalker said. "Layer by layer he's healing his fear."

"Jason, can you come out?" Wendy asked. "I want to talk to you."

He floated out of his body.

"You're making great progress," she told him.

"I heard," Jason said. "I *am* feeling better."

"So," Wendy said, "about this quantum mind business."

Jason smiled.

"How'd you learn about it?"

Bigger smile. "A friend of mine."

"Before you got sick?"

"Yeah."

"That's wild," she said.

From: tim@bob.com
To: lucidpath@tds.net
Sent: Friday, April 18
Subject: hi from abby

what's up? i thought i'd write you instead of tim this time. he types too slow. jason was looking good tonight. he looked really calm and chill - just kind of checking us out and looking around. my mom was there earlier and noticed the same thing. she said that he seems to have made some sort of switch. he isn't giving us those "please help me, where the hell am i" looks anymore. he seems a lot more at peace with what's going on. and he is moving his legs around. that makes me really happy because i have been saying that i just want him to move his legs, and then that was the first thing he did for me tonight. i was really worried about that before. it was sort of my mantra, "i just want him to move his legs," and now he is. so i'm really stoked. before his legs looked so sad lying there all sad looking not moving for weeks and weeks even when we tickled his feet. it really bothered me. guess i need a new mantra. so we are all pretty excited. it was definitely a good day for jason. oh, and he was breathing off the vent and his heart rate stayed nice and low. everything was just nice and calm. he just looked good - no more panicking or anxiety. and i loved seeing those legs move like that! i tell ya. it was exactly what i had been asking for.

one more thing - Jason had this friend who was on the board at his school named stuart. – he's a well-known ufo researcher and he knows a little about everything. my brother was crazy about this guy. you should try to contact him. he's really interesting and maybe he knows about jason's connection to the quantum mind stuff.

happy travels – a

From: Stuart@mesa.com
To: lucidpath@tds.net
Sent: Saturday, April 26
Subject: quantum Jason

Hi Wendy,

I am very happy to communicate with you about Jason. How is he? I miss him.

Jason and I first spoke about the Quantum Mind in front of the UACT School, (where I had just lectured) while we were talking about his music and the possibility that angels, aliens, and earthly spirits were affected by his music, through the doorway of intention. I do recall being intoxicated by our communication, as it is not very often that humans, (particularly humans of youth) are interested in the topic, let alone invigorate the concept.

He seemed to know a lot about it, be it naturally, intuitively, or scholastically... he was prepared to apply it in his own life, in his own supra-conscience.

In fact, personally I never felt that he was in danger. Please don't take this the wrong way. It was very sad what happened to him, from a medical point of view, and I would not want it to happen to him or anyone that I know. But... I never sensed that his soul, the true essence of Jason, was in danger of losing his being, his mind, or his spirit. He was somehow still connected, and he still is. I can learn a lot from him.

Warm Regards, Stuart

13

Jason stayed in his body for longer periods of time. It was becoming familiar. Still strange, but more familiar. To him it was kind of like the first week at a new job when you know you're supposed to be there, but don't quite feel comfortable enough to whistle in the hallway.

Buffalo Bill was never far away. He always showed up when Jason was most in need. Jason found great comfort in his company. The feeling was mutual. Bill found himself visiting Jason even when he wasn't in need.

"Hi Jason," Buffalo Bill said one day. "Need a lifeguard?"

"Come on Billy Boy," Jason said. "I'm doing much better. I haven't taken a swim in the sea of anxiety in quite a while. My worries have evolved. They've sprouted legs and crawled on to the shores of pain and discomfort."

"Very poetic," Bill said with a snort.

"Why, thank you," Jason said.

"I'm happy to see that you're feeling better," Bill said.

"Me too."

Bill's black lips spread into a wide toothy smile. "Perhaps the worst is over."

"On a good day, like today," Jason said, "I can see that in a twisted way being in a coma has given me the chance to face my fear of death. Until I got sick I don't think I realized how much the fear was fucking with my life."

"Jason," called a distant voice, "Jason, it's Wendy. Can you come out?"

Jason flew out of his body and was greeted by Wendy and two animals he'd never seen before.

"Hi," Jason said. "I see you brought some new friends with you."

"This is Adamson," Wendy said gesturing to a large white winged horse. On top of Adamson sat a white-faced capuchin monkey. "And this is Thelonius Monkey."

"Jazz fan?" Jason asked the monkey.

Thelonius winked at him.

Wendy rolled her eyes and turned to Jason. "Are you ready for some hard-core healing?"

"More hard-core than I've already been through?"

"Well, different," she said. "Deeper. If you're up for it we can catch your lost soul parts."

"What are you talking about?"

"It's big medicine," she said. "During trauma people can lose parts of their soul."

"Where do they go?"

"They hide out in the spirit world… confused, lost."

Wendy looked over at Adamson and Thelonius Monkey. "These guys," she continued, "are part of a special team of helpers who are brilliant at finding lost soul parts. Once they find them, the parts are invited back so that they can be reunited with the core soul."

"I must be getting used to all this crazy talk because what you're saying kinda makes sense," Jason said with a grin.

"It does make sense, doesn't it?" she said.

"Maybe I don't have any missing parts."

"I think everyone has soul loss. Some worse than others. Being on this planet… being human… it's a tough gig. We all get traumatized at one time or another. What I've found is that the more of your soul that's missing, the more difficult life is. You never really feel like yourself. No passion. No spark. It's like you're running on fumes energetically, emotionally, mentally and physically. You can't experience life fully."

"So it's kind of like listening to music while wearing ear plugs," he said.

"Exactly," Wendy said.

Mama, the Inuit spirit helper appeared.

"Is it time to bring the little one home?" Mama asked Wendy.

"There's only one part of my soul missing?" Jason asked.

"At least one," she said. "We've already met him. Get some cookies and milk ready Jason. We'll be back soon."

"Cookies sound good," Jason said.

In the next moment, Jason's hospital room transformed into an extraordinary garden surrounded by towering redwood trees and filled with flowers. Everything glowed as if illuminated from within. A small waterfall fed a winding brook. Jason's body was lying on a thick slab of stone, which sat under what looked like a Japanese pagoda. Moments later, the otherworldly landscape morphed back into Jason's hospital room. Wendy, the soul retrievers and the serene garden disappeared from view.

Adamson spread his great wings and took flight into the ethers. He led the group through the darkness toward a pinpoint of light in the distance. It seemed far away, but they were there in seconds. They found Little Jason playing video games in the log cabin Mama created for him.

"Hi Jason," Wendy said. "Where are your protectors?"

Without taking his eyes off the game, Little Jason motioned over his right shoulder where Spiderman, Wolverine, the Power Rangers and ET came into focus.

"I see you've been enjoying your magic," Mama said in a soft voice that pulled Little Jason's attention away from the screen. "You can play again later," she told him, "but now we need to talk about important things."

Little Jason nodded. Thelonius Monkey climbed into his lap and pinched the small boy's cheeks making him giggle.

"Would you like to go back, little one?" Mama asked.

"Back where?"

"To your body," Mama clarified.

He shrugged. "It's scary there. I like it here."

"I know you feel scared," Mama said, her melodic voice seemed to wrap him in the softest blanket of ease. "But feelings come and go. Who you really are, that never changes. Do you know who you really are Jason?"

He shook his head. Thelonius mimicked him.

Mama took Little Jason's face in her hands and whispered. "You… are a superhero."

Then she touched her forehead and nose to his and breathed into him.

Jason smiled. "I'm a superhero?"

Thelonius jumped up and posed with his hands on his hips. He wore a red cape, a black mask to conceal his identity, and in the middle of his chest, in big blue sparkling letters, were the initials TM.

"Hmmm," Mama said. "I think you are the bravest of all superheroes."

"Like Luke Skywalker?" Jason asked.

"Braver," Mama said. "I will call you Little Dream Wizard."

"Dream lizard?" Jason said.

"No, sweet one," Mama laughed, "wizard."

"I like wizards!" Jason said. "I'm really a wizard?"

"You can make magic happen just by wishing it so. That's what wizards do."

The boy glanced over to his protectors with a look that said, "Did you hear that? I'm one of you."

"Now that you know how powerful and brave you are," Mama said, "are you ready to go back?"

Little Jason bit his lip and shrugged.

"Much time has passed," Mama said. "Did you know that you're a grown-up now?

Little Jason's expression brightened.

"And Big Jason was telling me how much he misses you. He told me that it's just not as much fun without you."

"A grown-up?" Little Jason said. "You mean I can stay up as late as I want and I can drive a car?"

"Yes, you can do all those things," Mama said. "But right now Big Jason is very sick and needs to get better. He needs your magic to do this. Would you like to help?"

The boy's eyes filled with purpose. He nodded.

Thelonius jumped up and down, screeching with delight.

Mama placed Little Jason on Adamson's back and Thelonius hopped up after him. With a stomp of his hoof, Adamson flew off into the darkness leaving a trail of silver light behind them.

They arrived at the strange garden where Jason's comatose body was still lying on the stone slab. Mama lifted Little Jason off of Adamson and kneeled in front of him. She looked deep in his eyes, embraced him, and then whispered, "It's time, Little Dream Wizard."

Big Jason came out of his body and stood next to Wendy. He looked at the little version of himself and his eyes filled. *I remember you.* Little Jason ran up to him and jumped into his arms. They squeezed each other until they couldn't breathe. Big Jason buried his face in the little boy's neck.

"I'm here to help you get better," Little Jason said to him.

"I'm glad you're back," Jason said as he mussed Little Jason's hair. "We'll get through this." The little boy nodded and placed his head on Big Jason's heart, and melted into him.

He stood in silence with his eyes closed until the merge was complete and his dreambody became more solid.

"Thank you," Jason said.

Mama smiled and bowed her head slightly before disappearing.

Jason turned to Wendy. "That was intense."

"Need a nap?" Wendy joked.

"Actually I feel like playing a video game," he said. "Tetris. I haven't thought about playing that game in years."

There was movement on the other side of the brook that caught Jason's attention. He looked over and saw a group of little bearded men wearing pointy red hats.

"Are those leprechauns?" Jason asked in disbelief.

"No, garden gnomes," Wendy said. "I wouldn't say leprechaun too loudly around them. You'll piss them off."

"What are they doing?"

"Playing poker, I think," she said.

"Poker."

"Yeah, poker. They take care of this place."

"What is this place?"

"It's my garden. This is the place I've created in the dreamtime to do shamanic work."

"How come I've never seen it before?"

"I don't know," Wendy said. "Maybe because you're more relaxed you're able to perceive it better?" She got quiet for a moment. "It's strange. When I come here to meet with you, I actually see more of my garden than your hospital room. And you seem to see more of your hospital room than my garden." She shook her head. "Crazy. Two realities at once."

"Maybe a nap would be good," he said.

From: tim@bob.com

To: lucidpath@tds.net

Sent: Thursday, May 01

Subject: hello

one of these days i've got to get my own e-mail account, but for now i'll use tim's.

i've been able to spend more time with jason lately. i had been super busy for a few days and i wasn't able to be there as much as i wanted to. he's well, i'd like to think. he is communicating with me a lot more now. unfortunately the physical therapist put this arm brace on his left arm which is his most expressive hand and i think he really hates it. it's better obviously for him long term because he holds his hand and his arm in this really bad contorted position. i took it off while i was there and man did he clamp on to my hand right away. i was talking to him and he was even nodding his head a few times to a few questions. i feel pretty connected to him. at one point he was just looking at me and he had this totally pure little smile on his face, like he was remembering something funny. no joke. and i said to him, what are you thinking about, an inside joke? and he squeezed my hand a few times and nodded his head a bit and was still smiling at me. and then i think he had to cough, or something distracting happened. it was so funny? i think that's the first time i've ever been positive he smiled.

take care - abby

14

J ason's dreambody stuck a marshmallow on the end of a long stick and handed it to Little Jason who placed it in the twisting flames of the campfire.

"I'm convinced," Jason said glancing up at the black desert sky, "that there's life out there." When his eyes adjusted to the darkness above, millions of stars came into focus.

"What's your fascination with space creatures?" Buffalo Bill asked. The firelight danced in the crevasses of Bill's wooly brown face.

"I don't know," Jason replied. "It gives me hope, I guess. There's got to be a more advanced race of beings out there who can teach us more about the universe. I really want to explore – "

"Where no man has gone before," crooned a mocking voice.

Jason turned to see someone he vaguely knew from somewhere, maybe high school. Whoever he was, the guy was obnoxious.

"Fuck you," Jason said, upset that his private conversation with Bill had been interrupted.

"Sorry Captain Kirk," said the obnoxious guy.

"Now boys," said a giant panda bear who sat twirling an impaled fish over the fire. Her wispy voice was soft and feminine.

"I think aliens are a manifestation of man's fear," Obnoxious Guy said snidely.

"Definitely, if you look at the way they're portrayed in the media," Jason said. "That's how the government keeps the masses in check. It's so obvious. They want to keep us afraid." Jason eye-balled the obnoxious guy. "But that doesn't mean aliens don't exist. I think it's pretty ignorant to say they don't exist."

Wendy appeared and stood eavesdropping in the darkness outside the firelight.

"I once saw a space creature," Buffalo Bill said.

They all looked blankly at the enormous buffalo.

"Back when I was alive and wandering through the plains of what is now Wyoming," he continued. "I was milling about with my herd when all of a sudden a white sun appeared in the sky. We panicked and a stampede ensued."

"Would you say there was 'panda' monium?" Obnoxious Guy asked, throwing a cheesy grin in the panda's direction.

"That's really very funny," the panda said in a flat voice.

"What do you know about humor?" challenged Obnoxious Guy. "You're a freakin' panda– "

"Hey, knock it off," Jason said to the loathsome, obnoxious guy. "Don't pick fights with the panda bear. Alright? Shit."

"Leave her alone," said Little Jason flicking a melted marshmallow at the intolerable guy.

"Alright little man," the hateful, obnoxious, loathsome guy said. "I'll stop."

Jason was annoyed. *I guess since I'm in a coma, anyone can just show up in my dream and say whatever they want.*

"Hi everyone," Wendy said, stepping into the firelight.

As soon as Jason's attention focused on Wendy, the campfire scene faded and they were back in Jason's hospital room.

"I just wanted to check in on you," Wendy said.

"I'm doing okay, I guess," Jason said.

"So… who's the panda?" Wendy asked.

Jason sighed, "I have no clue. She just showed up." He smiled. "I've stopped questioning what happens anymore. If a panda wants to hang out at my pretend campfire with various versions of me, a talking Buffalo named Bill, and an obnoxious guy I barely know from high school, then so be it."

Wendy looked over at Jason's body and noticed it was sitting upright in the bed, looking very alert.

"I wish I could lie on my side," Jason said. "I hate not being able to move the way I want to. I'm also really hungry. I can't wait to eat real food again."

Images of French fries, tacos, and ice cream appeared in the air in front of them.

"At the rate you're going," Wendy said, "you'll be hittin' the drive-through windows in no time. I can't believe how much progress you've made in such a short time."

"Are you kidding?" he said. "You ask me, I'm way behind. Getting better is taking for-fucking-ever."

"I'm sure it feels slow to everyone – you, your family, your friends," Wendy said. "But remember, two months ago you were out of commission. You weren't breathing or swallowing on your own. And now look at you."

They looked at Jason's body, still seated in the hospital bed, his brow furrowed as he gazed at a game show on the TV.

"Your body seems more aware then I've ever seen it."

"Yeah, I guess," Jason said.

"Well, I think you're doing great. I've gotta go to a meeting. I'll see you next time," she said as she faded from view.

Wendy's attention shifted back to her garden. She made her way over to the pagoda structure where a small fire was burning. The Helpers, seated on soft cushions around the fire, were waiting for her. This was their meeting place.

"Have I thanked you lately for everything you're doing?" Wendy asked as she took a seat by the fire.

The Helpers nodded and smiled.

"Jason's pretty frustrated with how slow his healing is going," Wendy relayed.

"We're aware of his frustration," Oshira said.

"This may be difficult for him to understand," Raventalker added, the firelight dancing on her painted face, "but Jason's illness is a gift. Not only is he facing his tremendous fear of physical death, but everyone connected to him will be forever changed because of what he's going through.

"Of course," she continued, "this is true for some more than others. Before Jason got sick, everyone in his life, including Jason himself, was going about the very predictable routines of their lives… living each day as if the next day was a given."

"It's disturbing how drastically life can change in the blink of an eye," Wendy added.

Raventalker nodded. "Jason's family and friends… they ask, 'why did this happen?' The people in his life are struggling and searching now.

They're trying to make sense of this seemingly horrible turn of events."

One of the garden gnomes entered the pagoda carrying several logs. He grumbled as he tended the fire.

"Some," she explained, "will become angry and cynical. They'll run from their fear, escaping into distraction."

Raventalker paused, a gentle smile on her face. "Others will dig deep inside themselves and uncover a strength that they didn't know they had. And because of that, they'll cherish life and their relationships more."

Raventalker's words rolled around in Wendy's mind until they found resting places in the gaps of her understanding.

"So Jason's illness is giving everyone the same opportunity," she concluded, "but not everyone's going to take advantage of it."

The Helpers grinned, pleased that she understood.

"I know my experiences with Jason have changed *me*," she said. "I hope you don't take this the wrong way, but sometimes I feel like I'm making all this up." Wendy looked around the garden, her eyes catching sight of Thelonius Monkey, who was dressed like Santa Claus and hanging from a branch in a nearby maple tree.

Wendy shook her head, gestured to Thelonius, and said with a smile, "Need I say more?"

"He's a funny monkey," Li Ming giggled.

"I guess what I'm trying to say is…" Wendy paused and gathered her thoughts. "…having these visions, or whatever you want to call them, is a big leap for me. I was a card-carrying atheist since I was twelve. And now, by Western psychological standards, I'm delusional." She glanced back over at Thelonius, who blew her a kiss. "It's a lot for a girl like me to come to terms with."

Wendy stared into the fire, the flickering light catching hints of gold and copper in her long dark hair. "The more time I spend with you, the more I see how you impact people's lives in really positive, sometimes miraculous ways. I can feel my rational mind shrinking in response. And that can't be good!"

Wendy looked at the three Helpers. "Before I met Jason I really hoped that you, and all this," she said gesturing to the garden, "was real. Now I have no doubt."

"Aaah," Oshira said with delight, "you're learning to trust your experiences."

"Yeah, I guess I am," Wendy said with a smile.

Raventalker nodded. "Our work together will only get stronger."

....

From: Abby@bob.com

To: lucidpath@tds.net

Sent: Tuesday, May 20

Subject: hello again

hey – sorry i've been a little MIA.

i've been a little out of touch with jason lately . . . his new home is much further than the hospital and with my grandparents in town i'm trying to spend as much time with them as possible. it was good to see him over the weekend though. he definitely recognized me and he was smiling more than he used to. his roommate is a halupai indian – he is quadriplegic and draws and paints with his mouth. pretty amazing. he told someone in my family that jason is going to be alright – that he had a good feeling about jason. who knows, maybe he was just trying to make us feel better. i'd prefer to think he has the right idea.

we've got jason's whole ceiling decorated with posters of his that he seems to really like – at least he looks at them all the time. a few days before he got sick he made some artwork for school on his computer and gave it to a family friend. this guy was looking at it recently and it dawned on him that it said "Super Brain." so then i had it made into a poster and now it's on Jason's ceiling. pretty wild if you think about it. i wonder if jason had some sort of premonition?

my mom got info on the "rancho scale" which is how they measure cognitive functioning for people who have brain injuries. jason has been assessed at 2-3 by medical staff. here's the scale:

I.   NO RESPONSE

Person unresponsive to stimuli.

II.   GENERALIZED RESPONSE

Person reacts inconsistently and nonpurposefully to stimuli.
Responses are limited and often delayed.

III.   LOCALIZED RESPONSE

Person reacts specifically but inconsistently to stimuli. Responses are
related to type of stimulus presented, such as focusing on an object
visually or responding to sounds.

IV.   CONFUSED, AGITATED

Person is extremely agitated and in a high state of confusion. Shows
non-purposeful and aggressive behavior. Unable to fully cooperate
with his treatments due to short attention span. Maximal assistance
with self-care skills is needed.

V.   CONFUSED, INAPPROPRIATE, NON-AGITATED

Person is alert and can respond to simple commands on a more
consistent basis. Highly distractible and needs constant cueing to
attend to an activity. Memory is impaired with confusion regarding
past and present. The person can perform self-care activities with
assistance. May wander and need to be watched carefully.

VI.   CONFUSED, APPROPRIATE

Person shows goal directed behavior, but still needs direction from
staff. Follows simple tasks consistently and shows carryover for
relearned tasks. The person is more aware of his/her deficits and has
increased awareness of self, family and basic needs.

VII.   AUTOMATIC APPROPRIATE

Person appears oriented in home and hospital and goes through daily routine automatically. Shows carryover for new learning but still requires structure and supervision to ensure safety and good judgment. Able to initiate tasks in which he has an interest.

VIII.   PURPOSEFUL APPROPRIATE

Person is totally alert, oriented, and shows good recall of past and recent events. Independent in the home and in the community. Shows a decreased ability in certain areas but has learned to compensate.

we believe that Jason has moments of level 4 that the medical staff never sees.

hope all is well in jersey –

luv, abby

15

New Jersey...

When she woke the morning of May 27, Wendy was elated. Most of her dreams were unusual, but this particular dream was strangely ordinary: a slice of everyday life inserted into dreamtime.

In the dream, Wendy was in Arizona. She walked up to a picnic area somewhere in the desert. She guessed it was Phoenix because of all the grass. For some reason the residents of Phoenix are fond of grass.

It was a warm, beautiful day. There were no clouds – only miles and miles of pale blue sky. She had arrived at the park at which there was to be a big party. There were two people seated at one of the picnic tables waiting for her. She knew one of them was Jason's mother Carol. Wendy approached them and Carol stood up and gave her a big hug. Wendy glanced over to the other person and did a double take. It was Jason. He looked at her and smiled a big, shy smile. Wendy walked over to him. He braced himself on the table and pushed himself up slowly. He put his arms around her.

"Do you remember me?" she asked Jason.

"Yeah," he said, "I remember you."

Their eyes filled as they embraced. Neither could speak at that moment, but a lot was said.

Wendy pulled away and looked at Jason. He looked weak and gaunt. His brown hair was short and spiked with blonde highlights. He had grown a goatee that made him look a little older. But considering how much he'd been through, Wendy was amazed at how normal he looked. She could tell the whole experience had transformed him. He was calmer, more grounded. His anxiety was gone.

She hoped that the dream was a glimpse of the future. But even if it wasn't, the dream filled her with certainty. She knew he was going to be alright.

From: Carol@mesa.com

To: lucidpath@tds.net

Sent: Tuesday, May 27

Subject: your dream and an update

Hi Wendy,

Abby forwarded me your latest e-mail. What a wonderful dream!! I know I'm pretty anxious to meet you myself.

I thought I'd let you know how Jason is progressing. Today after physical therapy on his legs and arms we sat him up. He kept his head high for the first time – no trouble at all with the head! Whenever he would waiver in one direction he used his head to "right" the position. His physical therapist said that was reeeeeaaaaallll good. And when they sat him up in the Cadillac chair, he still held his head up high. While sitting in the chair he was switched to just moist air and the ventilator was turned off. I stayed with him for three hours after that and his breathing never changed. Not faster, not slower, not deeper, not shallower – no change. The respiratory tech was very impressed.

While in his chair, I introduced him to his roommate Henry (they typically can't see each other because both are immobile). Henry said hello to Jason. Jason looked around the room and then down at his body. He didn't have much of an expression on his face – not extreme anyway. He looked at his body for awhile and then leaned his head back. This was the first time I've seen him "look" at himself like that. It seemed to be a higher level of consciousness.

I noticed that Jason was squinting and closing his eyes. He had been doing that ever since I got there. So I told his nurse. She came in and asked him to open his eyes to look at her. He did so. She then asked him to track her from one side of the room to the other. Which he also did. She asked him if his eyes were burning and stinging. He nodded a definite "yes." She called the nurse practitioner who came right away. She determined that his eyes were dry and ordered some eye drops to help moisturize and lubricate. *This is new for Jason!!!* To follow so many commands and then answer a question!!! Landmark event: Jason responded and participated in his own care!!!!!!!

I've been telling Jason that the illness came in through one door and it leaves through the same door. I've been telling him that he is healed more than he knows and that he should experiment with his body and mind. It seems that he's been taking me up on my offer!

Love, Jason's mom Carol

16

J ason was restless. His dreambody drifted to the window and looked out. The parking lot was full. He watched as people got in and out of their cars and walked to and from the building. *They don't know how lucky they are.*

"What do you mean, lucky?" Jason's Indian guide asked as he came into view next to him.

"Hey," Jason said with a big smile, "where have you been?"

"I'm always with you," he answered. "Explain lucky please."

"Yeah, lucky," Jason sighed as he glanced back out the window. "Look at those people. How much do you think they appreciate being able to walk around, drive a car, eat food, or even fucking move their arms and legs?"

"How does that make them lucky? Because they're not you?"

"Yeah," he responded with a hint of venom, "because they're not me."

"It's important to remember that every human being suffers." The Indian looked deeply into Jason's eyes. "The suffering varies from person to person, but the end result is still pain. It's part of the experience of being human. You are not the only one to suffer."

"I guess that makes me lucky too." Sarcasm dripped from every word.

"It's not luck," the Indian said. "It's choice."

"I know, I know," Jason said. "I chose to be a prisoner in my body so I can evolve." His sarcasm was now forming a shallow pool at Jason's feet. "If one more person – or whatever – tells me I chose this shit, I will scream so loud that Satan, himself, will complain."

The Indian stifled a smile.

Jason put his head in his hands. *A fucking coma. I'm such an idiot.*

"I need to ask you a serious question," Jason said. "Am I going to end up like Stephen Hawking? Is that where I'm headed? Talking through a computer?"

"I don't know who Stephen Hawking is? Give me a moment." The Indian closed his eyes and focused. Within seconds he was given an image of a wheelchair-bound intellectual who couldn't speak.

"This man…he's done much with his life," the Indian said. "He's a well-respected scholar. Why would you not want to be like him?"

"Well, he's basically a brain in a useless body."

"I don't think Stephen Hawking sees it that way."

"I'm serious," Jason said. "Am I going to end up like him?"

"Your physical problems are different than his," the Indian answered.

"Yeah, well, that doesn't comfort me," Jason sighed.

"The biggest difference I can see between you and Stephen Hawking is that he accepts his situation."

"Man, you don't pull any punches, do you?"

The Indian looked quizzically at his fist and shrugged. He put his hand on Jason's shoulder. Jason immediately felt a wave of calm move through his dreambody.

"Man, that's nice," Jason said. "Why don't you come around more often and do that?"

"I do."

Jason smiled. "I just realized...I have no idea what your name is."

The Indian nodded. "You can call me Moves like Cat."

"Moves like Cat," repeated Jason. "Just rolls off your tongue, doesn't it?"

Moves like Cat stuck his tongue out in an attempt to see what Jason meant.

Jason laughed. "I didn't mean it literally. It's just an expression."

"I find your words very confusing."

"So," Jason said changing the subject, "how did you get your name?"

"When I was human I was a warrior. I was given the name because I could sneak up on others without them knowing I was there."

"I can see how that would be a helpful trait. Did you have to go to warrior school or something?"

"No," he answered. "Everyone has the spirit of the warrior in them. Some more than others, but everyone has it. It's what keeps you alive."

"I'm guessing the warrior in me is wanting overtime."

Moves like Cat was confused again. "Overtime?"

Jason laughed. "It's not important."

"If your warrior is motivated by fear, then his goal will be to coerce using force. If your warrior is motivated by love, then he will persuade with compassion."

"What do you think motivates my warrior?" Jason asked.

The spirit of a samurai dressed in armor and holding a sword appeared in front of them.

Jason looked at Moves like Cat. "Is he my warrior?"

Moves like Cat nodded.

The samurai readied his sword and leaped towards Jason with a growl as if to attack.

Jason jumped back. The image faded.

"I guess that answers my question," Jason said.

"When you can move from fear to love you can achieve mastery," Moves like Cat said. "You have a powerful intellect, young warrior. Your brain is filled with glorious theories and ideas. But you lack wisdom. Wisdom comes from experience. And to have experiences you need to take risks."

Jason wondered if he should be offended.

"Before you got sick you had confidence in your ideas, am I right?"

Jason took a deep breath. "Yeah, I thought I had it all figured out."

"And if you remember, you asked for this experience."

"Right. To face my fear of death."

"That's only part of the reason you're having this experience."

Jason looked confused. "What am I missing here?"

"You also longed for an opportunity to meet other life forms," Moves like Cat said. "Aliens, the angelic ones, spirits. Remember telling others how you wanted to experience these otherworldly entities? How you longed to understand…how did you put it…the quantum mind."

"Well yeah, but not like this."

"Your human self makes the wish, your Oversoul responds," Moves like Cat said. "How the wish is fulfilled is out of human hands."

Understanding dawned in Jason's eyes.

"You've been gifted with much time to spend with beings like me, yes?" Moves like Cat asked.

"I asked for this," Jason whispered. "You're right. I really did ask for this. I never connected my desire to meet aliens and stuff to this experience. But you're right. I've met all kinds of ethereal beings in coma land."

"Everything is beautifully orchestrated. Whether you're aware of it or not. There is purpose for everything."

From: Carol@mesa.com

To: lucidpath@tds.net

Sent: Sunday, June 1

Subject: WE FOUND THE PANDA BEAR!!!!

Wendy,

Remember the journey about Jason, a panda bear and other people sitting around a campfire talking about aliens????? A friend of ours had brought in a picture of a panda bear and taped it above Jason's bed. His respiratory therapist took it off the wall to look at it. She said she collects Panda Bears and then showed us one she had tattooed on her upper arm. She said she collects all things panda!!! She is a really good therapist (Jason's grandparents noted that she was the best therapist). She's been working w/ Jason more than she is required to. She's been teaching him how to use the speaking valve (still hasn't really talked) but tonight he said "miss my..." and never finished. Kim (the panda bear) also taught him something new – to bring up loogies and put them into the bonker-sucker. She said that she really likes Jason.

How strange is that?!!!!! We've thought all along he was in the right rehab center – there's so much hope and kindness there, and now the panda bear has shown herself!

17

Jason was in his body when Wendy and Raventalker arrived. He was focused on the television.

"Hey Jason," Wendy called.

Jason's dreambody drifted out of his physical one.

"How long have I been sick?" Jason asked.

Wendy did the math in her head. "Over five months."

"Really?" Jason said. "My whole concept of time is warped." He stared at his weak body laying propped up in the bed. His body's vacant eyes focused on the TV screen. His left arm was folded against his chest in an awkward, painful-looking position. His body had lost a lot of weight in those five months.

Jason shook his head.

"What's up?" Wendy asked, concerned.

"New doctors were in here talking about my 'condition'," Jason said. "It doesn't sound good at all. It looks like my brain is permanently damaged."

He sighed. "You know what frustrates me the most? I can't talk. I keep trying, but I can't get my mouth to work. I can make sounds, but no words."

Jason turned to Raventalker. "This is as good as it's going to get, isn't it?"

"Your life will never be the same Jason," Raventalker quietly responded. "But even with your... limitations, I believe you'll be able to find ways to communicate again."

Wendy gave Raventalker the death stare.

"Oh, that's fucking reassuring," Jason snapped.

Raventalker moved away from him, giving him space.

"I'm sorry," Jason said. "It's a lot to digest."

In the air before him, Jason saw a scene flicker into view. It was of himself when he had first arrived at the hospital. His body was hooked up to a ventilator and a slew of monitors. He was completely unresponsive.

Seeing this image was like a shot of cold air.

"I get your point," Jason said. "I've come a long way since then."

"I haven't seen it all," Wendy said, "but I've seen enough to know that when someone wants something badly enough they can beat some pretty impossible odds.

"I have this friend Chris who I haven't seen in probably ten years. I used to work with him when I was in college in Tucson.

"Around the time you got sick I started getting these e-mails from Chris's wife. She was sending them to a group of us, letting us know that he was in the hospital recovering from a pancreas transplant and that things weren't going well. His condition kept getting worse. I guess his body was rejecting the new pancreas."

The scene before Wendy and Jason shifted. They saw a different hospital room. The bed, which was surrounded by monitors and IVs, was enclosed by a thick, clear sheet of plastic.

"Is that Chris?" Jason asked.

Wendy nodded.

They watched as another version of Wendy appeared with Oshira, Raventalker and Li Ming.

The other version of Wendy pulled back the plastic and stepped closer to Chris's bed.

"Chris, can you hear me?" Wendy asked.

Chris's dreambody slipped out of his physical body.

"Who are you?" he asked.

"This is going to sound crazy," she said. "But we used to work together at the University of Arizona."

Chris looked closer. "You look familiar."

"I'm Wendy."

"Wendy?" Chris looked baffled. "What are you doing in my dream?"

"Remember how strange I was back then?"

Chris laughed. "You were definitely different."

"Well, I'm even stranger now. But we won't get into that. I'm here because I heard you were really sick and wanted to see if we could help."

Chris took in Wendy and the Helpers. "This is the strangest dream I've ever had. It seems so real."

"These folks here," Wendy said, gesturing to the Helpers, "they can help you heal if you want. But they won't help unless you ask."

"This is crazy," Chris said. He looked at his frail, discolored body in the bed. "I'm gonna die if something doesn't happen soon."

"Does that mean you want help?" asked Wendy.

"Yeah, I think so," Chris said shifting his gaze to Wendy. "Please help me."

The Helpers moved closer to the hospital bed to examine Chris's body. They saw a web of thin pulsing energy fibers circulating through his body. Everything looked to be flowing as it should except for a section in Chris's abdomen below his ribcage. The glowing strands of energy seemed to be avoiding a small area the size and shape of a sausage. The area was dark and had a single energy cord shooting out of it. The Helpers followed the cord and discovered that it led to a young man with dark hair who was standing on the other side of the hospital bed.

"That's mine," the young man said pointing to the pancreas in Chris's body. "I want it back."

Oshira gently approached the confused man. "Everything is okay," she said. "There's someone here for you."

Behind the young man appeared the spirits of two older people. They walked up to him and greeted him warmly. The young man recognized these two spirits as grandparents and embraced them. They spoke in hushed tones, and by the end of the conversation the young man seemed to understand that he was dead.

The Helpers told him that if he wanted to go with his loved ones he'd have to sever his connection to his physical body. He nodded and accepted the knife they offered him. Without hesitation the young man cut the energy cord connecting him to his pancreas. He turned to his grandparents and smiled as the three of them faded from view.

Li Ming integrated the energy in Chris's body to the energy of the donor's pancreas. Everything was flowing normally by the end of the healing.

"Damn," Jason said as the holographic vision faded. "Did it work?"

"About twenty-four hours later I got an e-mail saying that the doctors didn't know why… ," Wendy said exaggerating a wink, "but Chris's counts were improving. He was getting better.

"I know Chris's situation is completely different, but I wanted to show you – "

"I know," he interrupted. "I appreciate it." He looked as though his psyche was brimming. "Look, I've got a lot to think about."

"Sure," she said, "we'll get going then."

The scene shifted. Wendy and Raventalker sat next to the fire in Wendy's garden.

"So that's it?" Wendy asked. "He's not gonna get better?"

"We did all we could," Raventalker said softly.

Wendy's disappointment enveloped her like a heavy wool blanket.

"Some things are out of our hands," Raventalker explained. "Jason's circumstances reveal the difference between healing and curing." She looked at the fire and then at Wendy. "Everyone can be healed, but not everyone can be cured."

Raventalker watched as Wendy grasped the meaning of her words. "Please be assured," she continued, "that everything is unfolding for Jason as it should. Sometimes an Oversoul chooses very difficult life circumstances for itself.

"The lesson for those of us trying to be of service to Jason is to trust that there's a reason why things happen the way they do. And for Jason, the reason is between him and his Oversoul."

"What's the point then? Why do any of this?"

"Go back in your mind to our first encounters with Jason," Raventalker prompted. "What's been Jason's primary goal since we met him?"

Wendy stared at the fire and considered the question.

"To stay alive," she answered. "He didn't want to die."

"That's right. He's alive because your connection to him has allowed us to work with him and keep him alive. And because he's still alive he's been given the opportunity to heal his fear of death." Raventalker paused and smiled. "*That's* the point."

Wendy nodded. "I understand. I guess I was hoping for a happy ending."

"A full recovery."

"Yeah, I admit it. I wanted a miracle," Wendy said with a sheepish smile. "But clearly it's not up to me."

Raventalker's gaze locked on Wendy's. "Would you really want that kind of power?"

From: Carol@mesa.com

To: lucidpath@tds.net

Sent: Thursday, July 10

Subject: July 9 – Jason

I just got back from visiting Jason and I saw something that Abby saw!!!! It is truly amazing. Today his eyes were so bright and so Jason. His eyes have been through a lot of changes during his illness and today – they are *him*. I also figured out his "yes." He looks to his right and then back at you. It's very calculated and deliberate. Of course "no" is a quick shake of the head. I was so excited that we were actually communicating!!!! And also today he was intently watching me as I set up some things in his new room – I believe he is back!!!!

He's been struggling so much lately – between pneumonia and pluresy – in and out of the ER. We've all been up and down.

But today . . .

What a beautiful day!!

Will write again soon!

18

Jason's body was propped upright in the hospital bed. He stared at his left hand as if it were his mortal enemy. *Move, damn it! Come on.* His left elbow was clutched to his side. His clenched fist bent downward in an awkward position across his chest. *Give me a thumb's up you motherfucking piece of shit… come on, you can do this. It's not brain surgery.* His thumb separated from his fist slightly. He stared at his thumb as if trying to will its movement with his gaze. *Come on, you motherfucker.* His thumb lifted another inch. *That's right. That's what I'm talking about!*

"You know your thumb's going to have low self-esteem if you keep talking to it like that," Wendy said.

Jason's dreambody separated from his physical body. "When did you get here?"

"About two motherfucker's ago," she replied.

"Doing the simplest things takes all I've got. Did you see my thumb move? I'm actually quite proud of myself," Jason said. "I feel like I'm making progress."

"Hard work always pays off."

Raventalker, Oshira and Li Ming appeared.

"Then let's get to work," Raventalker said with a smile.

Li Ming moved next to Jason's body. He wore a deep red robe with long bell-like sleeves. He ran his hands over Jason's head and revealed a patch of slimy darkness at the base of Jason's skull, right above his neck. Li Ming scooped the dark gunk out of Jason's brain with two slender fingers and disposed of it in a bowl of water.

From his robe he retrieved two glowing rose-colored needles. Li Ming skillfully worked the needles as if knitting filaments of bright energy. When he was done he had created a pliable grid of light fibers that he carefully inserted into the damaged area of Jason's brain.

Li Ming looked at Jason's dreambody and giggled. "Your brain looks pretty now, yes?"

Jason smiled and said, "Yeah, real pretty. Thanks!"

Oshira glided over to Jason's body. She felt around the crown of his head for an edge and peeled back a thin, cloudy membrane that stuck to Jason's body like skin. She balled it up and threw it in the bowl of water that Li Ming had used.

What's that?

"She took off a layer of sleep," Wendy said.

"Man, that's cool," he said. "I wish I thought of that. Maybe I'd be out of coma land by now."

"This is your dream, Jason," Raventalker said.

Wendy cleared her throat. "Except for the gnomes and monkey. Doesn't seem fair to lay them on you."

"I thought you said I'm not dreaming. That this is really happening."

"I'm not talking about the dreams you have when you're sleeping," Raventalker said. "I'm talking about the dreaming of life. Everything in this dream represents a part of you. Everything." She looked pointedly at Wendy. "Even the gnomes."

They looked over to where the gnomes were gathered. They were sitting around a wooden table, smoking cherry tobacco out of long, narrow pipes. One of the gnomes turned to Jason, Wendy, and the Helpers, shook his raised fist at them, and grumbled.

Wendy looked at Jason. "You know, you should really get a handle on your gnomes. They're pretty rude."

Just then a fat white duck with a square head and bloodshot eyes waddled toward them. He was smoking a cigar and humming. As he shuffled by he started singing with a gruff Brooklyn accent. "Merrily, merrily, merrily, merrily... Life is but a dream."

After the duck passed, Jason asked, "I dreamed that?"

"Nope. He's one of mine too," Wendy admitted. "His name is Smelly." She pointed to her head and timidly shrugged.

"Whose dream is this?" Jason asked.

"Ah, now that's the question, isn't it?" Oshira answered, grinning.

Jason looked to Wendy for support.

"If you figure it out," Wendy said, "let me know."

From: Carol@mesa.com
To: lucidpath@tds.net
Sent: Sunday, August 24
Subject: Jason at home Aug. 23

Yesterday was a big day for us! Jason came home for a visit!!! After five and half months Jason came home for a few hours. It was quite the event! Jason especially liked posing for pictures – he's always been a ham! Abby got out the video camera and he really put on the pose! He liked everything about being home – and when it was time to go he got a little upset about having to go back to the rehab center. But we all assured him that he's coming home for visits every week, until he can come home for good.

He was exhausted as you can well imagine. Jason's dad, Bruce, was exhausted too. He had to go up and get Jason, wait two hours for the ride, come here, (the wait here was about one hour for them to be picked up), ride back, and then come home. It was an all day thing for Bruce. Jason was sound asleep before they got him back into bed. I was exhausted from pure adrenaline – I was soooooo excited!! I was worried a little that Jason wouldn't be able to tolerate the ride because everything would be moving so fast, but he did ok with that.

Attached is a picture of Jason at home. Notice we are doing "thumbs up."

And it started with a thumb . . .

Love, Carol

19

"Hey Bill," Jason called out. "You there?"

He heard a snort behind him.

"There you are," Jason said to the buffalo. "You got a minute?"

"I have nothing but time," Bill said. "You're looking well."

"Yeah, I'm feeling much better. That's why I wanted to talk to you. I can't figure out what's changed."

Bill moved closer to Jason's dreambody. Jason could feel Bill's breath as the buffalo's eyes penetrated him. A gentle calm enveloped Jason. Bill's breathing slowed and Jason felt himself lulled into its rhythm, until Bill abruptly let out a snort and broke the spell.

"I see you've found it," Bill said.

"Found what?" Jason asked. "My sanity?"

"No," Bill said. "Trust."

"Maybe I'm just used to all this now."

"It's there. I can see it," Bill said with a confirming grunt. "Your fear... your anxiety. It's under control."

Jason evaluated his level of anxiety. "Yeah," he said. "I guess it is."

"When you can trust, there's nothing to fear."

"Maybe you're right."

"Of course I'm right."

Jason rolled his eyes and smirked. "Geez, and it only took months of being in a coma to figure out that death isn't a one-way ticket into an existential wonderland of nothingness. But it's becoming painfully clear that this was the only way I was going to get it."

"But you *did* get it," Bill said with a theatrical bow of his head. "Bravo, my friend. Bravo!"

Jason jokingly bowed back. "Thank you. Thank you. You're too kind. I couldn't have done it without my friends in coma land – "

Jason stopped and looked to his left. He heard the sound of distant drumming. "I think Wendy's coming."

"Hey you," Wendy said as she came into view in front of Jason. She did a double take. "Man, you look good. New haircut?"

"No, actually I had my colors done," Jason said. "I'm an autumn."

"That's what it is!" she said. "Fall colors suit you."

Her gaze took on a playful, mysterious air. "So, I have this idea. You game?"

"Sure," he answered. "Why not?" Jason looked at Bill, exaggerated a wink, and said, "I trust you."

"Okay then," she said, not understanding the private joke between Bill and Jason. "Here's the plan. All you have to do is think about something you don't like about yourself. Something that no longer serves you, that you'd like to see die."

"I can do that," Jason said closing his eyes.

"Now invite this part of you to show itself."

They heard a tiny squeak and looked down. A cute little grey mouse scurried in circles at their feet.

Jason pointed. "That's my fear of death."

The mouse stopped and looked up at them. Without warning, it morphed into a cartoon mouse and bared its teeth at them as if it were a lion. Its fangs were fierce and freakishly immense and dripping with saliva. It let out a vicious roar.

The mouse transformed into a rat that was trapped in a wooden maze. The panic-stricken rat raced through the passageways, desperate to find a way out.

"That's what I used to think being dead was like," Jason said.

"No wonder you were so afraid to die. Existing like that," Wendy said pointing at the maze, "would completely suck."

They watched the rat run through corridor after corridor.

"Okay, this is torture," Wendy said. "How would you like to put the poor thing out of its misery?"

Jason decided to set a trap using a glass jar and some cheese. "I think I'll suffocate him." He looked to Wendy for approval.

"Hey," Wendy said, "it's your dream." She stepped back.

The rat followed its nose to the cheese and quickly crawled into the jar. Jason picked up the jar and looked inside. When his face was inches away, the rat morphed back into the intimidating cartoon mouse. It glared at Jason with tiny black eyes, bared its enormous fangs, and growled. Jason jerked his head back and screwed the lid shut.

For the mouse's funeral, Jason built a pyre out of twigs. He placed the dead mouse on its deathbed and set the pyre on fire. Hands clasped loosely in front of him, he observed a moment of silence and watched as the flames consumed his fear of death.

The sound of primal drumming broke the silence and Jason's somber ceremony quickly turned into a huge celebration with chanting and dancing. The Helpers, Moves like Cat, Buffalo Bill, the Panda Bear, and Little Jason stepped into the firelight. Everyone stomped and swayed around the fire, which had grown immense and powerful.

"How do you feel?" Wendy asked, joining him as he took in the scene.

"I guess I feel lighter," Jason answered. "A little –"

Jason was distracted by something moving in the sky. Gliding towards them was a triangular spacecraft adorned with glowing pale green lights. The spaceship landed not far from them and within seconds a hatch opened. Out walked three sinewy grayish-brown aliens with large heads and black almond-shaped eyes. They approached Jason in silence. The middle alien was carrying what looked like a folded white cloth. The alien trio stopped in front of Jason and stared at him for several long seconds before the alien in the middle presented the folded cloth to Jason with a slight bow. The trio turned around, went back to their ship, and flew off.

Jason looked quizzically at Wendy and then at the object in his hands. It was a t-shirt. He held it up and on the front was a picture of the cartoon mouse baring its teeth with the caption, *"I survived my fear of death."*

From: Carol@mesa.com
To: lucidpath@tds.net
Sent: Tuesday, November 25
Subject: killing the mouse

I read your journey with great interest – and a most unusual connection to report to you. Jason also slayed a mouse on Saturday night – the day before your journey!

We had brought Jason into the computer room so that we could see if he wanted to play solitaire. He doesn't fit at the computer desk properly yet because there's a drawer that prevents him from getting right up to the desk. Bruce had put the mouse on his lap on top of a lightweight piece of cardboard. It would be difficult for anyone to control a mouse like that – Jason tried for a few seconds and then got frustrated. So, he tossed the mouse on to the floor (which is what he does when he doesn't want something – off it goes). So then, it was like – "Jason you killed the mouse." My husband tried to fix it while Jason watched. We surmised that the mouse was dead.

Isn't that *bizarre*???!!??? That he chooses to make death a mouse that he slays – just after he killed the computer mouse?

Also – another strange connection. Saturday night we had company. Family friends of ours we have been close to for thirty years came over, and Jason was here to see them. My friend Lisa was telling me how the son of a close friend of hers died in a car accident the week prior. Jason had met the boy years ago although they were not great friends or anything. But Jason was listening to how the accident happened and how all three boys were killed instantly. Jason suddenly (although he waited until there was a slight lull in the conversation) mouthed the words "I almost died," so plainly that we both knew what he said. We were so amazed. Yes, Jason you almost died many times in the beginning of your illness, but you are strong and you made it – you're getting stronger every day.

This conversation about him almost dying had also been discussed between Jason and me a couple of days ago. He was really frustrated because I wanted him to do a puzzle. He threw the puzzle pieces and started mouthing something and crying. We talked about how simple things are hard for him right now. That I knew his mind was solid and I wanted him to do puzzles as therapy for his hand and eye coordination – not because I thought he was a baby (they're kid puzzles). And then we discussed how sick he had been up to this point. How we could not bear to lose him, and could not imagine our lives without him. That we wanted so desperately for him to live. I talked to him about how he almost died many times because of how sick he was. How we knew that if anyone could beat this virus – it was him because of how strong he was and because he was Jason.

Isn't that bizarre? That he chooses to get rid of his fear of death after we had those conversations in the days before your journey?

I am relieved that he handled that fear, that he chose to make death a mouse. I know that he is anxious to heal - that is obvious by the advances he makes daily. Every day in the last few weeks he's just adding more and more to the list of things he can do now. His frustration that it's not going fast enough for him is also a sign that he wants to heal.

Sunday evening when I was visiting with Jason he chose his position for the first time. The aides were getting him into bed and were trying to decide which side to put him on. They asked me which side and I said, "Let's ask Jason which side he prefers." Jason do you want to be on this side? He shakes his head no. The other side? Yes. I was impressed that he chose and so we had a discussion about how important it was for him to decide which way was most comfortable and to let his aides know. Then Debbie, the respiratory nurse came in. Debbie tried to wrestle his finger into the monitor. I told her that if she asks his permission he would let her conduct the test. Another tech had noticed earlier that, if he asked, Jason would let him do what he needed to do. But if he just came in and did it, Jason would pull the finger monitor off and toss it before the results could be gotten.

Yesterday, the day after your journey – but before we read it – Grandma noticed that he was more relaxed all day. He could relax his arm which is not a common thing. His occupational therapist reported yesterday that Jason didn't require more than one prompt to do a task she asked him to do. She said that it was his best therapy session yet! He also made a sound when one of the mothers said hello to him. In fact, yesterday he was making lots of sounds and mouthing lots of words – but no one could figure them out. It didn't stop Jason. His grandparents were so amazed with how alert and interactive he was yesterday.

So . . . that is what's going on here . . . Things are happening!!

Love, Carol

20

Moves like Cat was waiting for Wendy and Raventalker when they arrived. Jason was in his body and didn't notice them. He was focused on trying to move the fingers on his right hand.

"Our young friend has shifted his awareness from the world of spirit to the world of flesh," Moves like Cat noted.

Raventalker nodded in agreement. "He has a long, difficult road ahead of him."

"Does that mean our work is done?" Wendy asked.

Raventalker smiled. "For the time being."

Moves like Cat nodded. "He's a warrior now."

"I could feel you talking about me behind my back," Jason said as he glided out of his body. His dreambody was dimmer, harder to see.

"Technically," Wendy commented playfully, "we're not behind you."

"It's still impolite," Jason retorted with a grin.

"I think a certain mouse killer is leaving coma land," Wendy said gesturing to Jason's body.

"No turning back now," he added.

"I'm really proud of you," she told him.

"Maybe the idea of death doesn't send me into fits of panic anymore," Jason said glancing at his body on the bed. "But I'm in no hurry to die."

Jason shifted his gaze to Raventalker and looked deeply into her eyes. Raventalker bowed her head. He turned to Wendy who offered him a sad smile and open arms. Eyes welling, Jason embraced her and whispered, "Thank you."

Their farewell was interrupted by Thelonius Monkey, who noisily bounced by them donning a blond wig, red lipstick, and black sunglasses. He blew Jason a kiss before scurrying away, making everyone laugh.

"I'm gonna miss coma land," Jason acknowledged.

"I'll check in on you from time to time," Wendy said.

"I better get back now," he said awkwardly. "I've got a ton of fucking work to do if I ever want to eat real food again!"

"See you later," Wendy said as Jason disappeared into his rigid body.

21

New Jersey...

The rapid drumbeat playing on Wendy's stereo slowed down and gradually faded out. She opened her eyes and smiled.

22

Three years later…

J ason's dreambody reclined in the cockpit of a beautiful wooden sailboat. His right hand was draped lazily over the tiller, steering nowhere in particular.

The perfect breeze filled the sails and gently pulled the boat through silvery waves. The clear sky was illuminated by a brilliant, ethereal white light that sat port side on the horizon in the distance like an iridescent diamond.

Wendy appeared on the deck of the sailboat. Her hair, now streaked with a little gray, was cut at a severe angle, short in the back and long in the front. Jason noticed her, but showed no hint of recognition.

"You don't remember me, do you?" she asked.

He squinted at her. "You look familiar."

"I visited you after you got sick. In the hospital?"

Jason searched his memory.

"Coma land?" she said trying to jog his memory.

Recognition lit up his face. "Yeah, I remember now. You came with the monkey who likes to play dress up."

"That's right," Wendy said relieved that he had finally made the connection. "Thelonius."

Her eyes took in the otherworldly seascape. "You been out here a while?"

"Hard to say," he answered. "I think so. I couldn't take being in my body anymore."

"I heard you got real sick again."

"Yeah, it totally took the wind out of my sails," he said with a chuckle, looking at the billowing sails above him. "No, it hasn't been a fun experience for me or my family. Definitely not the rock star life I'd always dreamed of."

He looked out at the water. "But it's peaceful out here."

"I'm glad," she said.

"It's funny. I actually thought I could get better. Get my old life back. Make music again." He shot Wendy an impish grin. "Get my fifteen minutes. It might seem kinda lame, but I wanted my life to have an impact."

"That's not lame. I think we all kind of want that. But hey, you never know. Maybe your life will still have an impact, but in a different way," she said shooting him a mischievous smile back.

"What are you talking about?"

Wendy feigned ignorance.

"Fine," he said with a smirk. "Be that way."

Wendy took in the white light on the horizon. "Looks like you're winding down."

"I'm wasted," he said. "I've never been so tired."

"I can't believe you've hung in there as long as you have."

"Seemed important to try. For lots of reasons."

"It's good to see you, Jason," Wendy said.

He smiled. "Tell my family I'm okay."

Wendy nodded. "I'm sure our paths will cross again."

"Man, I hope so."

Wendy waved goodbye and smiled as she faded from view.

Moves like Cat and Buffalo Bill were with Jason in the cockpit of the sailboat. Little Jason sat crossed-legged on the deck in the front. Everyone seemed to take in the vast ocean vista with silent reverence. The brilliant white light was still off to left side of the boat, but it was much closer now.

Moves like Cat turned to Jason and placed his hand on his shoulder. The two communicated without words.

Buffalo Bill turned to Jason and offered a toothy grin.

Jason looked at Buffalo Bill, and then Moves like Cat, took a deep breath and nodded with certainty. He pushed the tiller to the right. The mainsail shifted in response and the boat turned, pointing directly at the white light.

Little Jason turned to Jason and smiled.

Jason's face was illuminated by the silvery light; his expression was calm, but his eyes revealed fierce determination.

author's note

For me, Jason's tale is truly a hero's journey.

My original motivation for writing *Slaying the Mouse* was to document an interesting case study in shamanic healing. However, as the narrative unfolded I discovered that Jason's story is a universal one. Jason not only confronted his paralyzing fear of death, but he walked right through the middle of it, and then bought it a beer.

One thing I've learned since being called to do this work is that each one of us is on a similar hero's journey. The obstacles we face may be different, but we all – at one time or another – have to engage with a part of ourselves that we'd prefer to keep locked away in the shadows of our psyche. It takes incredible courage to slay your mouse. But when you come out on the other side, you're not only healed, you're also brimming with the wisdom from that experience. And that's evolution.

So thank you Jason for sharing your journey with me. (As I write these words I can see his badass warrior self hanging out in the dreamtime… preparing for his next adventure.)

Happy trails my friend. Happy trails!!

about the author

A practicing psychotherapist for over fifteen years, Wendy Stofan Halley received her Master's degree in Clinical Psychology from Pepperdine University in 1995 and her Bachelor's degree in Interdisciplinary Studies from the University of Arizona in Tucson in 1992. Wendy has an active Shamanic teaching and healing practice working with people from all over the country.

She is also the author of the children's book *Inside Out* (Illumination Arts, Inc.) and a workbook/audio CD entitled *The Magical Path: Conscious Dreaming Exercises for Healing & Growth* that teaches readers how to access the spiritual realms for their own healing and evolution.

Wendy lives in central Vermont with her husband, John, and their dog friends Maggie, Omar, and everyone's favorite wiener dog, Maynard.

Visit her website www.lucidpath.com

To contact Wendy or Maynard, send an email to

lucidpath@tds.net

Praise for Wendy Halley's children's book
Inside Out

"Inside Out is a beautiful story that will remind children of what they already know. If all of us could live our lives this way, the world would be a much better place – full of peace, harmony, laughter and love."

Deepak Chopra

Author, *How to Know God*

"A thoroughly delightful book that is destined to become a classic. Inside Out will nurture your child's soul and help preserve their connection to spirit. Wendy Halley is to be commended as she has created very good medicine indeed."

Hank Wesselman, PhD

Author, *Spiritwalker Trilogy, The Journey to the Sacred Garden* and *Spirit Medicine*

"Inside Out is a captivating tale that reminds us all of the beautiful shiny spirits we truly are! A story for kids and adults alike. Children will jump on clouds along with Karly and Natasha. And adults will have fun remembering that they too can walk on the moon and be shiny and new. We loved it!"

Louisa and Rick Clerici

Authors, *Sparks from the Fire of Time*